KU-216-185

Driving
Theory
Test
Questions

REVISED

Driving
Theory
Test
Questions
REVISED

Including the questions and answers
valid for tests taken from 28 July 1997

Published by **BSM**
in association with
Virgin Publishing

First published in the UK in 1997 by
The British School of Motoring Ltd
81/87 Hartfield Road
Wimbledon
LONDON SW19 3TJ

Second printing 1997

Copyright © 1997 The British School of Motoring Ltd

All rights reserved. No part of this publication may be reproduced,
stored in a retrieval system, or transmitted, in any form or by any
means, electronic, mechanical, photocopying, recording or otherwise,
without the prior written permission of the copyright owners.

The questions contained herein are Crown copyright material
reproduced under licence from the Controller of HMSO and
the Driving Standards Agency.

ISBN 0 7535 0129 5

Cover picture and cartoons by Marc Lacey

Design, typesetting and reprographics by Prima Creative Services

Printed in Germany by Roto Stalling

Contents

Mark one ans

a   use only your sidelights
b   always use rear fog lights
c   always use your headlights
d   use headlights only in bad weather

b   you flash
overtaking

c   your rear fog ligh
on

d   you have switche
full bea

Q 209

Which TWO of the following are
correct? When overtaking at night you
should

Mark two answers

a   be careful because you
less

b   wait until a bend s
the oncoming

c   sound your horn twice
moving out

d   put your headlights on f
of bends in the ro

Foreword

Driving is an enjoyable and valuable life skill which is why every year nearly a million new learner drivers take to the road, each one of them with one clear aim. This aim is almost certainly the same as yours – to gain their full driving licence.

There is no substitute for practical experience when learning to drive. The best way to gain this is by taking lessons with a good professional driving instructor who uses the most up-to-date teaching techniques in a modern, dual-controlled car. However, it has always been equally important to prepare for your driving lessons and, since the introduction of the Theory Test, this is doubly true.

Driving Theory Test Questions contains the revised set (valid from July 1997) of official Driving Standards Agency questions which are currently published and which may be

included in the actual examination.

This book is an ideal study aid which allows you to test and revise your knowledge. It has been designed for use in conjunction with its companion volumes, *Pass Your Driving Theory Test* and *Pass Your Driving Test*. *Driving Theory Test Questions* allows you to check your level of knowledge by presenting you with real examination questions. The questions are set out under topic headings, and as you work through each section you will prove to yourself that you not only understand what you have learnt, but can demonstrate this by answering the question correctly.

In doing so, you will gradually boost your confidence and thereby recognise when you are ready to take and pass your Theory Test.

Your driving instructor will help you to plan your studies and ensure that you fully understand why the knowledge you acquire is essential to keep you safe on the road, as well as to take you past that first all important hurdle of passing your Theory Test.

There are no short cuts to becoming a safe and competent motorist, but that does not mean that you cannot enjoy yourself while learning.

Driving Theory Test Questions and its companion volumes, will, I hope, bring the Theory Test alive and make it relevant, and at the same time it should also help you develop your driving skills.

In over 85 years of teaching people to drive, BSM instructors have helped millions of people pass their driving test. In my view, *Driving Theory Test Questions* completes the best set of books available to help you make the most of your driving lessons and ensure that you prepare for both the theory and practical parts of your driving test in a structured and positive way.

Keith Cameron
Head of Road Safety Policy

Keith Cameron is one of Britain's leading authorities on motoring and driver education. He has held a number of senior positions within the Department of Transport; up to March 1992 he was Chief Driving Examiner with responsibility for all UK driving tests.

Introduction

The driving test was first introduced to the UK back in 1935. Since that time millions of people have passed the driving test and gained their motoring freedom, many taught by BSM instructors. Despite the substantial increase in road traffic, the driving test has hardly changed in all that time – at least until the last few years. Reverse parking was introduced as a practical test exercise in 1991, and in 1995 the decision was made to bring in a separate written test.

Most of Europe has already been operating a separate theory test for some time. The new British test has been developed to satisfy European Community Regulations and to bring us more into line with our European counterparts.

The Theory Test is now here to stay and in order to become a qualified driver you must now pass the theory as well as the practical driving test.

Driving Theory Test Questions contains the official Driving Standards Agency questions which are currently published and which may be included in the actual examination. That means there are a lot of questions in this book (609 in fact), but when you take your Theory Test, you won't be expected to answer all of them! Your paper will only have 35 questions for you to answer.

I am sure your main aim is to pass the Theory Test. Nevertheless, I strongly urge you to do more than simply attempt to learn the answers parrot fashion. Not only will you find such a method of learning very tedious, you will also miss out on the chance to understand the significance of the information you are learning and make use of it when you practise with your instructor.

The list on page 11 may seem daunting, but you can be completely confident that this book and its companion volumes, *Pass Your Driving Theory Test* and *Pass Your Driving Test*, cover each of the topic areas in detail.

Car and Motorcycle Theory Test Topics

Before each heading below, you will see the code S1, S2, S3 or S4. This indicates in which of the four sections of *Pass Your Driving Theory Test* you will find the topic covered.

MANDATORY TOPICS

S1 – Importance of alertness
Consideration, anticipation, observation, awareness, distraction, boredom.

S1 – Attitudes to other road users
Consideration, close following, courtesy, priority.

S1 – Knowledge of safe distances between vehicles, braking distances etc. (Conditions)
Safety margins and effect of bad weather and road surface conditions, visibility.

S1 – Impairment
Knowledge of reaction times and effects on driving behaviour of alcohol, fatigue, medication, drugs, stress, ill-health, ageing, sensory impairment (including eyesight).

S1 – Perception
Information processing, attention, scanning, identification of hazards, time to detect hazards, fixation, interpretation.

S1 – Judgement and decision-making
Appropriate action, interpretation, reaction time, speed, distance.

S2 – Risk factors associated with different road users
Children, pedestrians, disabled people, cyclists, elderly drivers, motorcyclists, new drivers/lack of traffic experience.

S2 – Risk factors associated with different road conditions
Own vehicle handling. Effects of: weather, road conditions, time of day (darkness), lighting, traffic calming, speed.

S2 – Behaviour in an accident
Rules on how to behave in case of an accident. Use of first aid kit and other first aid precautions, setting warning device and raising alarm, police reporting procedures, witness responsibilities, regulations.

S3 – Characteristics and statutory requirements of different types of roads
● Limitations on motorways: speed limits, lane discipline, stopping, lighting.
● Limitations on other types of road: speed limits, parking, clearways, lighting.

S3 – Road signs and traffic regulations
Road traffic regulations regarding road signs, markings, signals, rights of way and speed limits.

S4 – Administrative documents
Rules on administrative documents required for use of vehicles.

S4 – Safety factors relating to the vehicle and persons carried
Vehicle loading, stability, towing, regulations.

OPTIONAL TOPICS (Select one)

S4 – Mechanical aspects
How to detect the most common mechanical faults, defects that can affect safety, understanding of implications.

S4 – Vehicle safety equipment
Use of safety equipment (seat belts etc).

S4 – The environment
Rules on vehicle use in relation to the environment, emissions, fuel consumption, pollution (including noise), regulations.

Driving Theory Test Questions

Alertness

Q001

When turning your car in the road you should

Mark one answer

- a   overhang the kerb
- b   use a driveway if possible
- c   check all around for other road users
- d   keep your hand on the handbrake throughout

Q002

To move off safely from a parked position you should

Mark one answer

- a   signal if other drivers will need to slow down
- b   NOT look round if there is a parked vehicle close in front of you
- c   give a hand signal as well as using your indicators
- d   use your mirrors and look round for a final check

Q003

What, according to *The Highway Code*, do the letters MSM mean?

Mark one answer

- a   Mirror, signal, manoeuvre
- b   Manoeuvre, signal, mirror
- c   Mirror, speed, manoeuvre
- d   Manoeuvre, speed, mirror

Q004

What is the safest way to brake?

Mark one answer

- a   Brake lightly, then harder as you begin to stop, then ease off just before stopping.
- b   Brake hard, put your gear lever into neutral and pull your handbrake on just before stopping
- c   Brake lightly, push your clutch pedal down and pull your handbrake on just before stopping
- d   Put your gear lever into neutral, brake hard, then ease off just before stopping

Q005

You are driving on a wet road. You have to stop your vehicle in an emergency. You should

Mark one answer

- a   apply the handbrake and footbrake together
- b   keep both hands on the wheel
- c   select reverse gear
- d   give an arm signal

Q006

When following a large vehicle you should keep well back because

Mark one answer

- a   it allows the driver to see you in his mirrors
- b   it helps the large vehicle to stop more easily
- c   it allows you to corner more quickly
- d   it helps you keep out of the wind

Q007

As you approach this bridge you should

Mark three answers

○ a move into the middle of the road to get a better view
○ b slow down
○ c get over the bridge as quickly as possible
○ d consider using your horn
○ e find another route
○ f beware of pedestrians

Q008

You wish to overtake a long, slow-moving vehicle on a busy road. You should

Mark one answer

○ a wait behind until the driver waves you past
○ b flash your headlights for the oncoming traffic to give way
○ c follow it closely and keep moving out to see the road ahead
○ d keep well back until you can see that it is clear

Q009

In which of these situations should you avoid overtaking?

Mark one answer

○ a Just after a bend
○ b In a one-way street
○ c On a 30 mph road
○ d Approaching a dip in the road

Q010

You are driving at night and are dazzled by the headlights of an oncoming car. You should

Mark one answer

○ a slow down or stop
○ b close your eyes
○ c flash your headlights
○ d pull down the sun visor

Q011

You should only use a hand-held telephone when

Mark one answer

○ a your vehicle has an automatic gear change
○ b driving at low speeds
○ c you have stopped at a safe place
○ d travelling on minor roads

Q012

You are driving a vehicle fitted with a hand-held telephone. To answer the telephone you MUST

Mark one answer

- a   find a safe place to stop
- b   reduce your speed
- c   steer the car with one hand
- d   be particularly careful at junctions

Answers and Explanations

Q001   **c**

Q002   **d**

Q003   **a**

Q004   **a** Braking lightly at first and then harder reduces the risk of skidding. Easing off the brakes just before you stop avoids stopping with a jolt.

Q005   **b** This helps you maintain control of your car.

Q006   **a**

Q007   **b, d, f**

Q008   **d**

Q009   **d** You cannot see if a vehicle coming towards you is hidden by the dip.

Q010   **a**

Q011   **c**

Q012   **a** You must not use a hand-held telephone while you are driving.

Driving Theory Test Questions

Attitudes to Other Road Users

Driving Theory Test Questions

Q013

A pelican crossing that crosses the road in a STRAIGHT line and has a central island MUST be treated as

Mark one answer
- a   one crossing in daylight only
- b   one complete crossing
- c   two separate crossings
- d   two crossings during darkness

Q014

At a pelican crossing the flashing amber light means you should

Mark one answer
- a   stop, if you can do so safely
- b   give way to pedestrians already on the crossing
- c   stop and wait for the green light
- d   give way to pedestrians waiting to cross

Q015

What is meant by 'defensive' driving?

Mark one answer
- a   Being alert and thinking ahead
- b   Always driving slowly and gently
- c   Always letting others go first
- d   Pulling over for faster traffic

Q016

You are following a vehicle on a wet road. You should leave a time gap of at least

Mark one answer
- a   one second
- b   two seconds
- c   three seconds
- d   four seconds

Q017

You are approaching a pelican crossing. The amber light is flashing. You must

Mark one answer
- a   give way to pedestrians who are crossing
- b   encourage pedestrians to cross
- c   not move until the green light appears
- d   stop even if the crossing is clear

Q018

When should you beckon pedestrians to cross the road?

Mark one answer
- a   At pedestrian crossings
- b   At no time
- c   At junctions
- d   At school crossings

Q019

You are driving towards a zebra crossing. Pedestrians are waiting to cross. You should

Mark one answer
- a   give way to the elderly and infirm only
- b   slow down and prepare to stop
- c   use your headlamps to indicate they can cross
- d   wave at them to cross the road

Q020

You have stopped at a pedestrian crossing.
To allow pedestrians to cross you should

Mark one answer

○ a   wait until they have crossed
○ b   edge your vehicle forward slowly
○ c   wait, revving your engine
○ d   signal to pedestrians to cross

Q021

You stop for pedestrians waiting to cross
at a zebra crossing. They do not start to
cross. What should you do?

Mark one answer

○ a   Be patient and wait
○ b   Sound your horn
○ c   Drive on
○ d   Wave them to cross

Q022

You could use the 'Two-Second Rule'

Mark one answer

○ a   before restarting the engine after
       it's stalled
○ b   to keep a safe gap from the vehicle
       in front
○ c   before using the 'mirror, signal,
       manoeuvre' routine
○ d   when emerging on wet roads

Q023

A two-second gap between yourself and
the car in front is sufficient when
conditions are

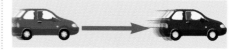

Mark one answer

○ a   wet
○ b   good
○ c   damp
○ d   foggy

Q024

'Tailgating' means

Mark one answer

○ a   using the rear door of a
       hatchback car
○ b   reversing into a parking space
○ c   following another vehicle
       too closely
○ d   driving with rear fog lights on

Q025

You are driving on a clear night. There is
a steady stream of oncoming traffic.
The national speed limit applies. Which
lights should you use?

Mark one answer

○ a   Full beam headlights
○ b   Sidelights
○ c   Dipped headlights
○ d   Fog lights

Q026

Following a large goods vehicle too closely is dangerous because

Mark one answer

- a your field of vision is seriously reduced
- b slipstreaming will reduce wind effect
- c your engine will overheat
- d your brakes need a constant cooling effect

Q027

When are you allowed to exceed the maximum speed limit?

Mark one answer

- a Between midnight and 6 am
- b Never
- c When overtaking
- d When the road's clear

Q028

While driving you approach a large puddle that's close to the left-hand kerb. Pedestrians are close to the water. You should

Mark two answers

- a ignore the puddle
- b brake suddenly and sound your horn
- c slow down before the puddle
- d try to avoid splashing the pedestrians
- e wave at the pedestrians to keep back

Q029

A long, heavily loaded lorry is taking a long time to overtake you. What should you do?

Mark one answer

- a Speed up
- b Slow down
- c Hold your speed
- d Change direction

Q030

You are in a line of traffic. The driver behind you is following very closely. What action should you take?

Mark one answer

- a Slow down, gradually increasing the gap between you and the vehicle in front
- b Ignore the following driver and continue to drive within the speed limit
- c Signal left and wave the following driver past
- d Move out wider to a position just left of the road's centre line

Q031

You are driving at the legal speed limit. A vehicle comes up quickly behind, flashing its headlamps. You should

Mark one answer

- a accelerate to maintain a gap behind you
- b touch the brakes to show your brake lights
- c maintain your speed and prevent the vehicle from overtaking
- d allow the vehicle to overtake

Q032

You are driving at the legal speed limit. A vehicle behind wants to overtake. Should you try to prevent the driver overtaking?

Mark one answer

- a No, unless it's safe to do so
- b Yes, because the other driver is acting dangerously
- c No, not at any time
- d Yes, because the other driver is breaking the law

Q033

You are driving in traffic at the speed limit for the road. The driver behind is trying to overtake. You should

Mark one answer

- a move closer to the car ahead, so the driver behind has no room to overtake
- b wave the driver behind to overtake when it is safe
- c keep a steady course and allow the driver behind to overtake
- d accelerate to get away from the driver behind

Q034

Which THREE of the following emergency vehicles will use blue flashing beacons?

Mark three answers

- a Motorway maintenance
- b Bomb disposal team
- c Blood transfusion
- d Police vehicle
- e Breakdown recovery vehicle

Q035

You are driving a slow-moving vehicle on a narrow road. When traffic wishes to overtake you should

Mark one answer

- a take no action
- b put your hazard warning lights on
- c stop immediately and wave them on
- d pull in safely as soon as you can do so

Q036

You are driving a slow-moving vehicle on a narrow winding road. You should

Mark one answer

- a keep well out to stop vehicles overtaking dangerously
- b wave following vehicles past you if you think they can overtake quickly
- c pull in safely when you can, to let following vehicles overtake
- d give a left signal when it is safe for vehicles to overtake you

Q037

Which THREE of these emergency services might have blue flashing beacons?

Mark three answers

- a Coastguard
- b Bomb disposal team
- c Gritting lorries
- d Animal ambulances
- e Mountain rescue
- f Doctors' cars

Q038

What type of emergency vehicle is fitted with a green flashing light?

Mark one answer

- a   Fire engine
- b   Road gritter
- c   Ambulance
- d   Doctor's car

Q039

A flashing green beacon on a vehicle means

Mark one answer

- a   police on non-urgent duties
- b   doctor on an emergency call
- c   road safety patrol operating
- d   gritting in progress

Q040

A vehicle has a flashing green light. What does this mean?

Mark one answer

- a   A doctor is answering an emergency call
- b   The vehicle is slow-moving
- c   It is a motorway police patrol vehicle
- d   A vehicle is carrying hazardous chemicals

Q041

What should you use your horn for?

Mark one answer

- a   To alert others to your presence
- b   To claim your right of way
- c   To greet other road users
- d   To signal your annoyance

Q042

Diamond-shaped signs give instructions to

Mark one answer

- a   tram drivers
- b   bus drivers
- c   lorry drivers
- d   taxi drivers

Q043

You are in a one-way street and want to turn right. You should position yourself

Mark one answer

- a   in the right-hand lane
- b   in the left-hand lane
- c   in either lane, depending on the traffic
- d   just left of the centre line

Q044

You should ONLY flash your headlamps to other road users

Mark one answer

- a   to show that you are giving way
- b   to show that you are about to reverse
- c   to tell them that you have right of way
- d   to let them know that you're there

Q045

A bus is stopped at a bus stop ahead of you. Its right-hand indicator is flashing. You should

Mark one answer

○ a flash your headlights and slow down

○ b slow down and give way if it is safe to do so

○ c sound your horn and keep going

○ d slow down and then sound your horn

Q046

A vehicle pulls out in front of you at a junction. What should you do?

Mark one answer

○ a Swerve past it and blow your horn

○ b Flash your headlights and drive up close behind

○ c Slow down and be ready to stop

○ d Accelerate past it immediately

Answers and Explanations

Q013   **b**

Q014   **b**

Q015   **a**

Q016   **d** In good conditions you should allow two seconds but on a wet road you double this to four.

Q017   **a** You must give way to pedestrians already on the crossing but may drive on if the crossing is clear.

Q018   **b** Pedestrians must decide for themselves when it is safe to cross.

Q019   **b** The word 'only' makes 'a' wrong and you should never flash or wave at pedestrians to cross.

Q020   **a**

Q021   **a** Pedestrians are naturally nervous and cautious at crossings, so allow them time. Only drive on if you are certain they do not intend to cross.

Q022   **b** A two-second time gap from the vehicle in front provides a safe gap in good conditions.

Q023   **b**

Q024   **c**

Q025   **c**

Q026   **a**

Q027   **b**

Q028   **c, d**

Q029   **b** By slowing down you allow the lorry to get past, which is the only safe option.

Q030   **a** By increasing the gap between you and the vehicle in front, you give yourself and the driver behind more room to stop should you need it.

Q031   **d** This is your only safe option.

Q032   **c** Even if other drivers are breaking the law or acting dangerously, you are likely to increase the danger if you try to prevent them overtaking.

Q033   **c**

Q034   **b, c, d**

Q035   **d**

Q036   **c** 'a' and 'b' are dangerous and 'd' is confusing. Other drivers might think you are stopping or turning left.

Q037   **a, b, e**

Q038   **d** Doctors on emergency call may display a flashing green light. Slow-moving vehicles have amber flashing lights. Police, fire and ambulance service vehicles have blue flashing lights.

Q039   **b**

Q040   **a**

Q041   **a**

Q042   **a**

Q043   **a** To turn right from a one-way street you normally position yourself in the right-hand lane.

Q044   **d** You should only flash your headlights to warn other road users that you are there.

Q045   **b** This eases congestion but the other answers could cause confusion.

Q046   **c** This is the only safe thing to do. The other answers are the actions of an aggressive driver.

Driving Theory Test Questions

Vehicle Defects, Safety Equipment and the Environment

Q047

Which of these, if allowed to get low, could cause an accident?

Mark one answer

- ○ a   Antifreeze level
- ● b   Brake fluid level
- ○ c   Battery water level
- ○ d   Radiator coolant level

Q048

The legal minimum depth of tread for car tyres over three-quarters of the breadth is

Mark one answer

- ○ a   2.5 mm
- ○ b   4 mm
- ○ c   1 mm
- ● d   1.6 mm

Q049

It is illegal to drive with tyres that

Mark one answer

- ● a   have a large deep cut in the side wall
- ○ b   have been bought second-hand
- ○ c   are of different makes
- ○ d   have painted walls

Q050

Which THREE does the law require you to keep in good condition?

Mark three answers

- ● a   Gears
- ● b   Clutch
- ● c   Headlights
- ● d   Windscreen
- ● e   Seat belts

Q051

Which FOUR of these must be in good working order for your car to be roadworthy?

Mark four answers

- ○ a   Temperature gauge
- ● b   Speedometer
- ○ c   Windscreen washers
- ● d   Windscreen wipers
- ● e   Oil warning light
- ● f   Horn

Q052

New petrol-engined cars must be fitted with catalytic converters. The reason for this is to

Mark one answer

- ○ a   control exhaust noise levels
- ○ b   prolong the life of the exhaust system
- ○ c   allow the exhaust system to be recycled
- ○ d   reduce harmful exhaust emissions

Q053

It is important that tyre pressures are correct. They should be checked at least

Mark one answer

- ○ a   once a week
- ○ b   every time the vehicle is serviced
- ○ c   every four weeks
- ○ d   every time the vehicle has an MOT test

Q054

Why should tyres be kept to the pressure the manufacturer tells you?

Mark one answer

- a   To keep the car the right height off the road
- b   To save wear on the engine
- c   To stop the car from sloping to one side
- d   To help prevent the car from skidding

Q055

Excessive or uneven tyre wear can be caused by faults in the

Mark two answers

- a   braking system
- b   suspension
- c   gearbox
- d   exhaust system

Q056

Driving with under-inflated tyres can affect

Mark two answers

- a   engine temperature
- b   fuel consumption
- c   braking
- d   oil pressure

Q057

The main cause of brake fade is

Mark one answer

- a   the brakes overheating
- b   air in the brake fluid
- c   oil on the brakes
- d   the brakes out of adjustment

Q058

What is the most important factor in avoiding running into the car in front?

Mark one answer

- a   Making sure your brakes are efficient
- b   Always driving at a steady speed
- c   Keeping the correct separation distance
- d   Having tyres that meet the legal requirements

Q059

Your vehicle pulls to one side when braking. You should

Mark one answer

- a   change the tyres around
- b   consult your garage as soon as possible
- c   pump the pedal when braking
- d   use your handbrake at the same time

Q060

If you notice a strong smell of petrol as you drive along you should

Mark one answer

- a   not worry, as it is only exhaust fumes
- b   carry on at a reduced speed
- c   expect it to stop in a few miles
- d   stop and investigate the problem

Q061

When are you allowed to drive if your brake lights DO NOT work?

Mark one answer

○ a   During the daytime
○ b   When going for an MOT test
○ c   At no time
○ d   In an emergency

Q062

When may you use hazard warning lights?

Mark one answer

○ a   To park alongside another car
○ b   To park on double yellow lines
○ c   When you are being towed
○ d   When you have broken down

Q063

What will reduce the risk of neck injury resulting from a collision?

Mark one answer

○ a   An air-sprung seat
○ b   Anti-lock brakes
○ c   A collapsible steering wheel
○ d   A properly adjusted head restraint

Q064

Why is it important that footwear is suitable for driving?

Mark one answer

○ a   To help you adjust your seat
○ b   To enable you to walk for assistance should you need to
○ c   To maintain control of the pedals
○ d   To prevent wear on the pedals

Q065

Hazard warning lights should be used when vehicles are

Mark one answer

○ a   broken down and causing an obstruction
○ b   faulty and moving slowly
○ c   being towed along a road
○ d   reversing into a side road

Q066

It is important to wear suitable shoes when you're driving. Why is this?

Mark one answer

○ a   To prevent wear on the pedals
○ b   To maintain control of the pedals
○ c   To enable you to adjust your seat
○ d   To enable you to walk for assistance if you break down

Q067

You must NOT sound your horn

Mark one answer

○ a   between 10 pm and 6 am in a built-up area
○ b   at any time in a built-up area
○ c   between 11.30 pm and 7 am in a built-up area
○ d   between 11.30 pm and 6 am on any road

Q068

A properly adjusted head restraint will

Mark one answer

- ○ a make you more comfortable
- ○ b help you to avoid neck injury
- ○ c help you to relax
- ○ d help you to maintain your driving position

Q069

You are carrying two children and their parents in your car. Who is responsible for seeing that the children wear seat belts?

Mark one answer

- ○ a The children's parents
- ○ b You
- ○ c The front-seat passenger
- ○ d The children

Q070

Car passengers MUST wear a seat belt if one is available, unless they are

Mark one answer

- ○ a under 14 years old
- ○ b under 1.5 metres (5 feet) in height
- ○ c sitting in the rear seat
- ○ d exempt for medical reasons

Q071

A car driver MUST ensure that seat belts are worn by

Mark one answer

- ○ a all front-seat passengers
- ○ b all passengers
- ○ c all rear-seat passengers
- ○ d children under 14

Q072

You are testing your suspension. You notice that your vehicle keeps bouncing when you press down on the front wing. What does this mean?

Mark one answer

- ○ a Worn tyres
- ○ b Tyres under-inflated
- ○ c Steering wheel not located centrally
- ○ d Worn shock absorbers

Q073

In which of these containers may you carry petrol in a motor vehicle?

Mark one answer

- ○ a
- ○ b Lighter Fuel
- ○ c SUPER OIL 15W40
- ○ d COLA

Q074

When should you NOT use your horn in a built-up area?

Mark one answer

- ○ a Between 8 pm and 8 am
- ○ b Between 9 pm and dawn
- ○ c Between dusk and 8 am
- ○ d Between 11.30 pm and 7 am

Q075

You cannot see clearly behind when reversing. What should you do?

Mark one answer

- ○ a   Open your window to look behind
- ○ b   Open the door and look behind
- ○ c   Look in the nearside mirror
- ○ d   Ask someone to guide you

Q076

What will cause high fuel consumption?

Mark one answer

- ○ a   Poor steering control
- ○ b   Accelerating around bends
- ○ c   Driving in high gears
- ○ d   Harsh braking and accelerating

Q077

When driving a car fitted with automatic transmission what would you use 'kick down' for?

Mark one answer

- ○ a   Cruise control
- ○ b   Quick acceleration
- ○ c   Slow braking
- ○ d   Fuel economy

Q078

What can cause heavy steering?

Mark one answer

- ○ a   Driving on ice
- ○ b   Badly worn brakes
- ○ c   Over-inflated tyres
- ○ d   Under-inflated tyres

Q079

It is essential that tyre pressures are checked regularly. When should this be done?

Mark one answer

- ○ a   After any lengthy journey
- ○ b   After driving at high speed
- ○ c   When tyres are hot
- ○ d   When tyres are cold

Answers and Explanations

Q047 **b** A low level of brake fluid may cause your brakes to fail

Q048 **d**

Q049 **a**

Q050 **c, d, e**

Q051 **b, c, d, f** These must, by law, be in good working order.

Q052 **d** This helps the car operate more efficiently and cause less air pollution. Only unleaded fuel may be used.

Q053 **a** Incorrect tyre pressures can affect the control and road holding of the vehicle and lead to excessive tyre wear.

Q054 **d** Incorrect tyre pressures add to the risk of skidding.

Q055 **a, b**

Q056 **b, c**

Q057 **a**

Q058 **c** 'c' is correct because of the words 'most important factor'; 'a' and 'd' obviously also help.

Q059 **b**

Q060 **d** Your car might catch fire if you drove on.

Q061 **c** It is a legal requirement to have brake lights that work.

Q062 **d** You should not use hazard warning lights when being towed so 'c' is wrong.

Q063 **d** If you are involved in an accident, the head restraint helps protect your neck from whiplash.

Q064 **c**

Q065 **a**

Q066 **b**

Q067 **c** The regulation only applies in a built up area.

Q068 **b**

Q069 **b** However, if someone over 14 years is in the car it is their own responsibility.

Q070 **d** All passengers, front and rear, must wear seat belts, if fitted, unless exempt for medical reasons.

Q071 **d** If passengers are under 14 it is the driver's responsibility to ensure they wear seat belts.

Q072 **d**

Q073 **a**

Q074 **d**

Q075 **d** If you cannot see properly you need to get someone to help.

Q076 **d** Harsh braking is one of the major causes of high fuel consumption.

Q077 **b** A short firm pressure right down on the gas pedal causes a quick change down to the next lower gear – useful, for example, when you need to overtake.

Q078 **d**

Q079 **d**

Driving Theory Test Questions

Weather and Road Conditions

Driving Theory Test Questions

Q080

Stopping in good conditions at 30 mph takes at least

Mark one answer

- a two car lengths
- ● b six car lengths
- c three car lengths
- d one car length

Q081

You are on a good, dry road surface and in a vehicle with good brakes and tyres. What is the shortest overall stopping distance at 40 mph?

Mark one answer

- ● a 23 metres (75 feet)
- b 96 metres (315 feet)
- c 53 metres (175 feet)
- d 36 metres (120 feet)

Q082

What is the braking distance at 50 mph?

Mark one answer

- a 55 metres (180 feet)
- b 24 metres (79 feet)
- c 14 metres (45 feet)
- ● d 38 metres (125 feet)

Q083

What is the shortest stopping distance at 70 mph?

Mark one answer

- a 53 metres (175 feet)
- ● b 60 metres (200 feet)
- c 73 metres (240 feet)
- d 96 metres (315 feet)

Q084

You are driving at 50 mph in good conditions. What would be your shortest stopping distance?

Mark one answer

- a 23 metres (75 feet)
- b 36 metres (120 feet)
- c 53 metres (175 feet)
- d 73 metres (240 feet)

Q085

You are travelling at 50 mph on a good, dry road. What is your overall stopping distance?

Mark one answer

- a 36 metres (120 feet)
- b 53 metres (175 feet)
- ● c 75 metres (245 feet)
- d 96 metres (315 feet)

Q086

What is the shortest overall stopping distance on a dry road from 60 mph?

Mark one answer

- a 53 metres (175 feet)
- b 58 metres (190 feet)
- c 73 metres (240 feet)
- d 96 metres (315 feet)

Q087

Your overall stopping distance will be much longer when driving

Mark one answer

- a   in the rain
- b   in fog
- c   at night
- d   in strong winds

Q088

You are on a fast, open road in good conditions. For safety, the distance between you and the vehicle in front should be

Mark one answer

- a   a two-second time gap
- b   one car length
- c   2 metres (6 feet 6 inches)
- d   two car lengths

Q089

What is the main reason why your stopping distance is longer after heavy rain?

Mark one answer

- a   You may not be able to see large puddles
- b   The brakes will be cold because they're wet
- c   Your tyres will have less grip on the road
- d   Water on the windscreen will blur your view of the road ahead

Q090

You are driving in heavy rain when your steering suddenly becomes very light. To get control again you must

Mark one answer

- a   brake firmly to reduce speed
- b   ease off the accelerator
- c   use the accelerator gently
- d   steer towards a dry part of the road

Q091

You are driving in heavy rain. Your steering suddenly becomes very light. You should

Mark one answer

- a   steer towards the side of the road
- b   apply gentle acceleration
- c   brake firmly to reduce speed
- d   ease off the accelerator

Q092

You have driven through a flood. What is the first thing you should do?

Mark one answer

- a   Stop and check the tyres
- b   Stop and dry the brakes
- c   Switch on your windscreen wipers
- d   Test your brakes

Q093

Braking distances on ice can be

Mark one answer

- a   twice the normal distance
- b   five times the normal distance
- c   seven times the normal distance
- d   ten times the normal distance

Q094

You are driving along a country road. You see this sign. AFTER dealing safely with the hazard you should always

Ford

Mark one answer

- a check your tyre pressures
- b switch on your hazard warning lights
- c switch on your rear fog lamps
- d test your brakes

Q095

Freezing conditions will affect the distance it takes you to come to a stop. You should expect stopping distances to increase by up to

Mark one answer

- a two times
- b five times
- c three times
- d ten times

Q096

Skidding is mainly caused by

Mark one answer

- a the weather
- b the driver
- c the vehicle
- d the road

Q097

When driving in icy conditions, the steering becomes light because the tyres

Mark one answer

- a have more grip on the road
- b are too soft
- c are too hard
- d have less grip on the road

Q098

You are driving in freezing conditions. Which TWO should you do when approaching a sharp bend?

Mark two answers

- a Accelerate into the bend
- b Slow down before you reach the bend
- c Gently apply your handbrake
- d Avoid sudden steering movements
- e Position towards the middle of the road

Q099

You are driving on an icy road. How can you avoid wheelspin?

Mark one answer

- a Drive at a slow speed in as high a gear as possible
- b Use the handbrake if the wheels start to slip
- c Brake gently and repeatedly
- d Drive in a low gear at all times

Q100

How can you avoid wheelspin when driving in freezing conditions?

Mark one answer

- a Stay in first gear all the time
- b Put on your handbrake if the wheels begin to slip
- c Drive in as high a gear as possible
- d Allow the vehicle to coast in neutral

Q101

You are driving in freezing conditions. What should you do when approaching a sharp left-hand bend?

Mark two answers

- a Slow down before you reach the bend
- b Gently apply your handbrake
- c Firmly use your footbrake
- d Coast into the bend
- e Avoid sudden steering movements

Q102

You are turning left on a slippery road. The back of your vehicle slides to the right. What should you do?

Mark one answer

- a Brake firmly and not turn the steering wheel
- b Steer carefully to the right
- c Steer carefully to the left
- d Brake firmly and steer to the left

Q103

You are turning left on a slippery road. The back of your vehicle slides to the right. You should

Mark one answer

- a brake firmly and not turn the steering wheel
- b steer carefully to the left
- c steer carefully to the right
- d brake firmly and steer to the left

Q104

You are braking on a wet road. Your vehicle begins to skid and you do not have anti-lock brakes. What's the first thing you should do?

Mark one answer

- a Quickly pull up the handbrake
- b Push harder on the brake pedal
- c Gently use the accelerator
- d Release the footbrake fully

Q105

How can you tell when you are driving over black ice?

Mark one answer

- a It is easier to brake
- b The noise from your tyres sounds louder
- c You see black ice on the road
- d Your steering feels light
- e Other vehicles will get out of the way

Q106

You are braking on a wet road. Your vehicle begins to skid. Your vehicle does not have anti-lock brakes. What is the FIRST thing you should do?

Mark one answer
- a Quickly pull up the handbrake
- b Release the footbrake fully
- c Push harder on the brake pedal
- d Gently use the accelerator

Q107

Coasting the vehicle

Mark one answer
- a improves the driver's control
- b makes steering easier
- c reduces the driver's control
- d uses more fuel

Q108

When driving in fog in daylight you should use

Mark one answer
- a sidelights
- b full beam headlights
- c hazard lights
- d dipped headlights

Q109

You're at a junction with limited visibility. You should

Mark one answer
- a inch forward, looking to the right
- b inch forward, looking to the left
- c inch forward, looking both ways
- d be ready to move off quickly

Q110

In very hot weather the road surface can get soft. Which TWO of the following will be affected most?

Mark two answers
- a The suspension
- b The steering
- c Braking
- d The windscreen

Q111

In windy conditions you need to take extra care when

Mark one answer
- a using the brakes
- b making a hill start
- c turning into a narrow road
- d passing pedal cyclists

Q112

You are on a long, downhill slope. What should you do to help control the speed of your vehicle?

Mark one answer
- a Grip the steering wheel tightly
- b Select neutral
- c Select a low gear
- d Put the clutch down

Q113

Your indicators may be difficult to see in bright sunlight. What should you do?

Mark one answer

- a   Put your indicator on earlier
- b   Give an arm signal as well as using your indicator
- c   Touch the brake several times to show the stop lamp
- d   Turn as quickly as you can

Q114

You are about to go down a steep hill. To control the speed of your vehicle you should

Mark one answer

- a   select a high gear and use the brakes carefully
- b   select a high gear and use the brakes firmly
- c   select a low gear and use the brakes carefully
- d   select a low gear and avoid using the brakes

Q115

You wish to park facing DOWNHILL. Which TWO of the following should you do?

Mark two answers

- a   Turn the steering wheel towards the kerb
- b   Park close to the bumper of another car
- c   Park with two wheels on the kerb
- d   Put the handbrake on firmly
- e   Turn the steering wheel away from the kerb

Q116

You are driving in a built-up area. You approach a speed hump. You should

Mark one answer

- a   move across to the left-hand side of the road
- b   wait for any pedestrians to cross
- c   slow your vehicle right down
- d   stop and check both pavements

Q117

When approaching a right-hand bend you should keep well to the left. Why is this?

Mark one answer

- a   It improves your view of the road
- b   To overcome the effect of the road's slope
- c   It lets faster traffic from behind overtake
- d   To be positioned safely if the vehicle skids

Q118

You are coming up to a right-hand bend. You should

Mark one answer

○ a   keep well to the left as it makes the bend faster

◉ b   keep well to the left for a better view around the bend

○ c   keep well to the right to avoid anything in the gutter

○ d   keep well to the right to make the bend less sharp

Q119

When driving in snow it's best to keep in as high a gear as possible. Why is this?

Mark one answer

○ a   To help you slow down quickly when you brake

○ b   So that wheelspin doesn't cause your engine to run too fast

○ c   To leave a lower gear available in case of wheelspin

○ d   To help to prevent wheelspin

Q080 b The diagram on the back cover of *The Highway Code* illustrates this.

Q081 d

Q082 d Note this is the braking distance. The overall stopping distance is further because you have to add 'thinking' distance.

Q083 d

Q084 c

Q085 b

Q086 c

Q087 a

Q088 a This is the 'two-second' rule.

Q089 c

Q090 b This problem is sometimes called aquaplaning. Your tyres build up a thin film of water between them and the road and lose all grip. The steering suddenly feels light and probably uncontrollable. The solution is to ease off the accelerator until you feel the tyres grip the road again.

Q091 d

Q092 d Your brakes may be wet. The first thing you should do is check them and then dry them.

Q093 d

Q094 d Drive slowly forwards with your left foot gently on the footbrake. This helps dry out the brakes.

Q095 d

Q096 b Skidding is usually caused by harsh braking, harsh acceleration or harsh steering – all actions of the driver. You are more likely to cause a skid in a poorly maintained car, in bad weather or on a poor road surface.

Q097 d

Q098 b, d Braking on an icy bend is extremely dangerous. It could cause your vehicle to spin.

Q099 a Wheel spin is caused by too much acceleration. The less grip the tyres have on the road, the more wheel spin is likely, and on icy roads the tyres have very little grip. A slow speed is essential and a high gear keeps the wheels turning more gently for the speed.

Q100 c

Q101 a, e

Q102 b Steer into a skid to correct it. Oversteering, however, could result in a skid in the opposite direction. Remember to remove the cause of the skid by coming off the pedals.

Q103 c

Q104 d Your first action must be to remove the cause of the skid.

Q105 d Black ice is normally invisible when you are driving. The tyres will lose grip with the road which will make the steering feel light.

Q106 b Note that the question asks for the first thing you should do, which is always to remove the cause of the skid – in this case braking. You would next need to re-apply the brakes more gently. 'c' is wrong because braking harder would increase the skid.

Q107 c Coasting means driving along with the clutch pedal down. This disconnects the engine and gears from the drive wheels of the car, so you have less control.

Q108 d Sidelights are not enough so 'a' is wrong. Full beam headlights tend to reflect back the fog, so 'b' is also incorrect.

Q109 c You cannot go until you can see that it is safe, so you need to inch forward until you can see clearly in both directions.

Q110 b, c

Q111 d In windy conditions cyclists are all too easily blown about and may wobble or steer off course.

Q112 c You should ideally have selected the lower gear before starting down the slope. Both 'b' and 'd' would be likely to make your car go faster as you would no longer be in any gear at all.

Q113 b

Q114 c A low gear will help control your speed, but on a steep hill you will also need your brakes.

Q115 a, d If the handbrake should fail, the car will roll into the kerb and not down the road.

Q116 c

Q117 a You can see further round the bend earlier if you keep to the left.

Q118 b

Q119 d

Driving Theory Test Questions

Hazard Perception

Q120

You see this sign on the rear of a slow-moving lorry that you want to pass. It is travelling in the middle of the road. You should

Mark one answer

- ○ a cautiously approach the lorry then pass on either side
- ○ b follow the lorry until you can leave the motorway
- ○ c wait on the hard shoulder until the lorry has stopped
- ○ d approach with care and keep to the left of the lorry

Q121

Where would you expect to see these markers?

Mark two answers

- ○ a On a motorway sign
- ○ b At the entrance to a narrow bridge
- ○ c On a large goods vehicle
- ○ d On a builder's skip placed on the road

Q122

What does this signal, from a police officer, mean to oncoming traffic?

Mark one answer

- ○ a Go ahead
- ○ b Stop
- ○ c Turn left
- ○ d Turn right

Q123

What is the main hazard shown in this picture?

Mark one answer

- ○ a Vehicles turning right
- ○ b Vehicles doing U-turns
- ○ c The cyclist crossing the road
- ○ d Parked cars around the corner

Q124

Which road user has caused a hazard?

Mark one answer

- a The parked car (arrowed A)
- b The pedestrian waiting to cross (arrowed B)
- c The moving car (arrowed C)
- d The car turning (arrowed D)

Q125

What should the driver of the car approaching the crossing do?

Mark one answer

- a Continue at the same speed
- b Sound the horn
- c Drive through quickly
- d Slow down and get ready to stop

Q126

What should the driver of the red car do?

Mark one answer

- a Wave the pedestrians who are waiting to cross
- b Wait for the pedestrian in the road to cross
- c Quickly drive behind the pedestrian in the road
- d Tell the pedestrian in the road she should not have crossed

Q127

What THREE things should the driver of the grey car be specially aware of?

Mark three answers

- a Pedestrians stepping out between cars
- b The bumpy road surface
- c Empty parking spaces
- d Other cars behind the grey car
- e Cars leaving parking spaces
- f Parked cars' doors opening

Q128

What should the driver of the red car (arrowed) do?

Mark one answer

- ○ a Sound the horn to tell other drivers where he is
- ○ b Squeeze through the gap
- ○ c Wave the driver of the white car to go on
- ◉ d Wait until the car blocking the way has moved

Q129

What should the driver of the grey car (arrowed) do?

Mark one answer

- ◉ a Cross if the way is clear
- ○ b Reverse out of the box junction
- ○ c Wait in the same place until the lights are green
- ○ d Wait until the lights are red then cross

Q130

What should the driver of a car coming up to this level crossing do?

Mark one answer

- ○ a Drive through quickly
- ◉ b Drive through carefully
- ○ c Stop before the barrier
- ○ d Switch on hazard warning lights

Q131

What are TWO main hazards a driver should be aware of when driving along this street?

Mark two answers

- ○ a Glare from the sun
- ◉ b Car doors opening suddenly
- ○ c Lack of road markings
- ○ d The headlights on parked cars being switched on
- ○ e Large goods vehicles
- ◉ f Children running out from between vehicles

Q132

What is the main hazard a driver should be aware of when following this cyclist?

Mark one answer

- ○ a The cyclist may move into the left gap and dismount
- ● b The cyclist may swerve out into the road
- ○ c The contents of the cyclist's carrier may fall onto the road
- ○ d The cyclist may wish to turn right at the end of the road

Q133

The driver of which car has caused a hazard?

Mark one answer

- ● a Car A
- ○ b Car B
- ○ c Car C
- ○ d Car D

Q134

When approaching a hazard your FIRST reaction should be to

Mark one answer

- ○ a use your footbrake
- ○ b change direction
- ● c release the accelerator
- ○ d check the mirrors

Q135

What is the main hazard the driver of the red car (arrowed) should be most aware of?

Mark one answer

- ○ a Glare from the sun may affect the driver's vision
- ○ b The black car may stop suddenly
- ● c The bus may move out into the road
- ○ d Oncoming vehicles will assume the driver is turning right

Q136

In heavy motorway traffic you're being followed closely by the vehicle behind. How can you lower the risk of an accident?

Mark one answer

- ☑ a   Increase your distance from the vehicle in front
- ○ b   Tap your foot on the brake pedal
- ○ c   Switch on your hazard lights
- ○ d   Move onto the hard shoulder and stop

Q137

You think the driver of the vehicle in front has forgotten to cancel his right indicator. You should

Mark one answer

- ○ a   sound your horn before overtaking
- ○ b   overtake on the left if there's room
- ○ c   flash your lights to alert the driver
- ○ d   stay behind and not overtake

Answers and Explanations

Q120   d
Q121   c, d
Q122   b
Q123   c
Q124   a
Q125   d
Q126   b
Q127   a, e, f
Q128   d
Q129   a
Q130   c
Q131   b, f
Q132   b
Q133   a
Q134   d Only then will you have the information you need to make a decision.
Q135   c
Q136   a
Q137   d

Impairment

Q138

To drive you must be able to read a
number plate from what distance?

Mark one answer

- ○ a   10 metres (33 feet)
- ○ b   15 metres (50 feet)
- ○ c   20.5 metres (67 feet)
- ○ d   205 metres (673 feet)

Q139

You find that you need glasses to read
vehicle number plates. When must you
wear them?

Mark one answer

- ○ a   Only in bad weather conditions
- ○ b   At all times when driving
- ○ c   Only when you think it necessary
- ○ d   Only in bad light or at night time

Q140

A driver can only read a number plate at
the required distance with glasses on.
The glasses should be worn

Mark one answer

- ○ a   all the time when driving
- ○ b   only when driving long distances
- ○ c   only when reversing
- ○ d   only in poor visibility

Q141

How does alcohol affect your driving?

Mark one answer

- ○ a   It speeds up your reactions
- ○ b   It increases your awareness
- ○ c   It improves your co-ordination
- ● d   It reduces your concentration

Q142

You're about to drive home. You can't find
the glasses you need to wear when
driving. You should

Mark one answer

- ○ a   drive home slowly, keeping to
       quiet roads
- ○ b   borrow a friend's glasses and drive
       home
- ○ c   drive home at night, so that the
       lights will help you
- ○ d   find a way of getting home
       without driving

Q143

Which THREE result from drinking alcohol
and driving?

Mark three answers

- ● a   Less control
- ○ b   A false sense of confidence
- ● c   Faster reactions
- ● d   Poor judgement of speed
- ○ e   Greater awareness of danger

Q144

A driver attends a social event.
What precaution should the driver take?

Mark one answer

- ○ a   Drink plenty of coffee after
       drinking alcohol
- ○ b   Avoid busy roads after drinking
       alcohol
- ○ c   Avoid drinking alcohol completely
- ○ d   Avoid drinking alcohol on an
       empty stomach

Q145

What are THREE ways that drinking alcohol can affect driving?

Mark three answers

- a It slows down your reactions
- b It reduces your co-ordination
- c It affects your judgement of speed
- d It reduces your confidence

Q146

When driving, what is the maximum legal level for alcohol in your blood?

Mark one answer

- a 50 mg per 100 ml
- b 60 mg per 100 ml
- c 80 mg per 100 ml
- d 90 mg per 100 ml

Q147

The maximum prison sentence for the offence of driving while unfit through drink and drugs is

Mark one answer

- a 12 months
- b 18 months
- c 6 months
- d 24 months

Q148

Which one of the following IS NOT affected by alcohol?

Mark one answer

- a Judgement of speed
- b Reaction time
- c Perception of colours
- d Co-ordination

Q149

Which THREE of these are likely effects of drinking alcohol on driving?

Mark three answers

- a Reduced co-ordination
- b Increased confidence
- c Poor judgement
- d Increased concentration
- e Faster reactions
- f Colour blindness

Q150

What advice should you give to a driver who has had a few alcoholic drinks at a party?

Mark one answer

- a Have a strong cup of coffee and then drive home
- b Drive home carefully and slowly
- c Wait a short while and then drive home
- d Go home by public transport

Q151

Your doctor has given you a course of medicine. Why should you ask if it is OK to drive?

Mark one answer

- a Drugs make you a better driver by quickening your reactions
- b You'll have to let your insurance company know about the medicine
- c Some types of medicine can cause your reactions to slow down
- d The medicine you take may affect your eyesight

Q152

The offence of causing death while driving under the influence of drink or drugs carries the maximum penalty of

Mark one answer

- ○ a 8 years' imprisonment
- ○ b 10 years' imprisonment
- ○ c 12 years' imprisonment
- ○ d 6 years' imprisonment

Q153

You are not sure if your cough medicine will affect your driving. What TWO things could you do?

Mark two answers

- ○ a Ask your doctor
- ○ b Check the medicine label
- ○ c Drive if you feel alright
- ○ d Ask a friend or relative for advice

Q154

You take some cough medicine given to you by a friend. What must you do before driving?

Mark one answer

- ○ a Drink some strong coffee
- ○ b Ask your friend if taking the medicine affected their driving
- ● c Check the label to see if the medicine will affect your driving
- ○ d Make a short journey to see if the medicine's affecting your driving

Q155

You have taken medication that may make you feel drowsy. Your friends tell you it is safe to drive. What should you do?

Mark one answer

- ○ a Take their advice and drive
- ○ b Ignore your friends' advice and do not drive
- ○ c Only drive if they come with you
- ○ d Drive for short distances only

Q156

You are taking drugs that are likely to affect your driving. What should you do?

Mark one answer

- ○ a Seek medical advice before driving
- ○ b Limit your driving to essential journeys
- ○ c Only drive if accompanied by a full licence-holder
- ○ d Drive only for short distances

Q157

If you are feeling tired it is best to stop as soon as you can. Until then you should

Mark one answer

- ○ a increase your speed to find a stopping place quickly
- ○ b ensure a supply of fresh air
- ○ c gently tap the steering wheel
- ○ d keep changing speed to improve concentration

Q158

Your reactions will be much slower when driving

Mark one answer

○ a   if tired
○ b   in fog
○ c   too quickly
○ d   in rain

Q159

You are driving on a motorway. You feel tired. You should

Mark one answer

○ a   carry on but drive slowly
○ b   leave the motorway at the next exit
○ c   complete your journey as quickly as possible
○ d   stop on the hard shoulder

Q160

You are planning to drive a long distance. Which THREE things will make the journey safer?

Mark three answers

○ a   Avoid travelling at night
◉ b   Ensure a supply of fresh air
○ c   Avoid motorways
○ d   Make stops for refreshments
○ e   Drive slowly

Q161

How often should you stop on a long journey?

Mark one answer

○ a   When you need petrol
○ b   At least every four hours
○ c   At least every two hours
○ d   When you need to eat

Q162

Which TWO things would help to keep you alert during a long journey?

Mark two answers

○ a   Finish your journey as fast as you can
○ b   Keep off the motorways and use country roads
○ c   Make sure that you get plenty of fresh air
○ d   Make regular stops for refreshments

Q163

Which THREE are likely to make you lose concentration while driving?

Mark three answers

◉ a   Looking at road maps
◉ b   Listening to loud music
○ c   Using your windscreen washers
○ d   Looking in your wing mirror
◉ e   Using a mobile phone

Q164

A driver pulls out of a side road in front of you. You have to brake hard. You should

Mark one answer

- a   ignore the error and stay calm
- b   flash your lights to show your annoyance
- c   sound your horn to show your annoyance
- d   overtake as soon as possible

Q165

A car driver pulls out causing you to brake. You should

Mark one answer

- a   keep calm and not retaliate
- b   overtake and sound your horn
- c   drive close behind and sound your horn
- d   flag the driver down and explain the mistake

Q166

Another driver does something that upsets you. You should

Mark one answer

- a   try not to react
- b   let them know how you feel
- c   flash your headlamps several times
- d   sound your horn

Q167

Another driver's behaviour has upset you. It may help if you

Mark one answer

- a   stop and take a break
- b   shout abusive language
- c   gesture to them with your hand
- d   follow their car, flashing your headlights

Answers and Explanations

Q138 c Glasses or contact lenses may be worn.

Q139 b If you need glasses to drive you must wear them whenever you are driving, so 'b' is correct.

Q140 a

Q141 d You may well feel, after drinking, that 'a', 'b' and 'c' are true, which is never correct but makes you dangerous.

Q142 d It is illegal to drive if you cannot satisfy the requirements of the eyesight test.

Q143 a, b, d

Q144 c The golden rule – if you intend to drive DO NOT DRINK ALCOHOL.

Q145 a, b c Drinking tends to falsely increase your confidence which makes 'd' wrong.

Q146 c 35 microgrammes per 100ml of breath, 80 milligrammes per 100ml of urine.

Q147 c

Q148 c

Q149 a, b, c

Q150 d The only sensible answer is don't drink and drive.

Q151 c The answer required is 'c' but do remember that 'd' is also possible, particularly if the medicine was related to an eye problem.

Q152 b

Q153 a, b

Q154 c

Q155 b

Q156 a A significant number of drugs, even those you can buy in the chemist, can affect your ability to drive. Sometimes a warning is given on the packet, but if in any doubt seek medical advice.

Q157 b

Q158 a

Q159 b If you feel tired you greatly increase your chances of having an accident. You must stop, but as you are on a motorway you cannot do this unless you leave at the next exit or find a service station before it.

Q160 a, b, d Fresh air and refreshment help keep you alert and you are more likely to be most able to concentrate during daylight hours.

Q161 c

Q162 c, d

Q163 a, b, e 'c' and 'd' are normal parts of the driving task.

Q164 a 'b', 'c' and 'd' can only make matters worse. So 'a' is correct. You should certainly stay calm and ignore the error in the sense of not reacting to it. Next time you may predict such an error before it happens and be able to stay safe without braking hard.

Q165 a

Q166 a However hard, the safest course is to try not to react and since the increase in road rage this is even more essential. Reacting tends to increase danger or raise the risk of violence.

Q167 a

Driving Theory Test Questions

Other Road Users

Q168

You are driving on a country road. What should you expect to see coming towards you on YOUR side of the road?

Mark one answer

- a Motorcycles
- b Bicycles
- c Horse riders
- d Pedestrians

Q169

Which sign means that there may be people walking along the road?

Mark one answer

- a
- b
- c
- d

Q170

What does this sign mean?

Mark one answer

- a Pedestrian crossing
- b Pedestrians in the road ahead
- c No pedestrians
- d Route for pedestrians

Q171

You are turning left into a side road. Pedestrians are crossing the road near the junction. You must

Mark one answer

- a wave them on
- b sound your horn
- c switch on your hazard lights
- d wait for them to cross

Q172

You are turning left at a junction. Pedestrians have started to cross the road. You should

Mark one answer

- a go on, giving them plenty of room
- b stop and wave at them to cross
- c blow your horn and proceed
- d give way to them

Q173

You are turning left from a main road into a side road. People are already crossing the road into which you're turning. You should

Mark one answer

- a   continue, as it is your right of way
- b   signal to them to continue crossing
- c   wait and allow them to cross
- d   sound your horn to warn them of your presence

Q174

You are at a road junction, turning into a minor road. There are pedestrians crossing the minor road. You should

Mark one answer

- a   stop and wave the pedestrians across
- b   sound your horn to let the pedestrians know that you are there
- c   give way to the pedestrians who are already crossing
- d   carry on; the pedestrians should give way to you

Q175

You want to reverse into a side road. You are not sure that the area behind your car is clear. What should you do?

Mark one answer

- a   Look through the rear window only
- b   Get out and check
- c   Check the mirrors only
- d   Carry on, assuming it's clear

Q176

You are about to reverse into a side road. A pedestrian wishes to cross behind you. You should

Mark one answer

- a   wave to the pedestrian to stop
- b   give way to the pedestrian
- c   wave to the pedestrian to cross
- d   reverse before the pedestrian starts to cross

Q177

You are reversing from a driveway and cannot see clearly. There are many pedestrians around. You should

Mark one answer

- a   continue whilst sounding your horn
- b   continue with your hazard lights on
- c   get someone to guide you
- d   continue; it is your right of way

Q178

You want to turn right from a junction but your view is restricted by parked vehicles. What should you do?

Mark one answer

- a Move out quickly, but be prepared to stop
- b Sound your horn and pull out if there is no reply
- c Stop, then move slowly forward until you have a clear view
- d Stop, get out and look along the main road to check

Q179

In which THREE places would parking your vehicle cause danger or obstruction to other road users?

Mark three answers

- a In front of a property entrance
- b At or near a bus stop
- c On your driveway
- d In a marked parking space
- e On the approach to a level crossing

Q180

What must a driver do at a pelican crossing when the amber light is flashing?

Mark one answer

- a Signal the pedestrian to cross
- b Always wait for the green light before proceeding
- c Give way to any pedestrians on the crossing
- d Wait for the red-and-amber light before proceeding

Q181

The approach to a zebra crossing is marked with zigzag lines.
Which TWO must you NOT do within the marked area?

Mark two answers

- a Overtake
- b Cross the lines
- c Drive at more than 10 mph
- d Park

Q182

What type of crossing is this?

Mark one answer

- a A zebra crossing
- b A pelican crossing
- c A puffin crossing
- d A toucan crossing

Q183

At toucan crossings

Mark two answers

- ○ a there is no flashing amber light
- ○ b cyclists are not permitted
- ○ c there is a continuously flashing amber beacon
- ○ d pedestrians and cyclists may cross
- ○ e you only stop if someone is waiting to cross

Q184

When may you stop on a pedestrian crossing?

Mark one answer

- ○ a Not at any time
- ○ b To avoid an accident
- ○ c When there's a queue of traffic in front of you
- ○ d Between the hours of 11 pm and 7 am

Q185

Look at this picture. What is the danger you should be most aware of?

Ice cream van
Child
Parked car

Mark one answer

- ○ a The ice cream van may move off
- ○ b The driver of the ice cream van may get out
- ○ c The car on the left may move off
- ○ d The child may run into the road

Q186

You are driving past parked cars. You notice a wheel of a bicycle sticking out between them. What should you do?

Mark one answer

- ○ a Accelerate past quickly and sound your horn
- ○ b Slow down and wave the cyclist across
- ○ c Brake sharply and flash your headlights
- ○ d Slow down and be prepared to stop for a cyclist

Q187

You are driving past a line of parked cars. You notice a ball bouncing out into the road ahead. What should you do?

CRU 332Y

Mark one answer

- ○ a Continue driving at the same speed and sound your horn
- ○ b Continue driving at the same speed and flash your headlights
- ○ c Slow down and be prepared to stop for children
- ○ d Stop and wave the children across to fetch their ball

Q188

What does this sign tell you?

Mark one answer
- a   No cycling
- b   Cycle route ahead
- c   Route for cycles only
- d   End of cycle route

Q189

What does this sign warn you to look for?

Mark one answer
- a   A school crossing patrol
- b   A pedestrian crossing
- c   A park
- d   School children

Q190

You see a pedestrian carrying a white stick. This shows that the person is

Mark one answer
- a   disabled
- b   deaf
- c   elderly
- d   blind

Q191

How will a school crossing patrol signal you to stop?

Mark one answer
- a   By pointing to children on the opposite pavement
- b   By displaying a red light
- c   By displaying a stop sign
- d   By giving you an arm signal

Q192

You see someone step into the road holding this sign. What must you do?

Mark one answer
- a   Slow down and look out for children
- b   Signal the person to cross
- c   Drive carefully round the person
- d   Pull up before the person

Q193

You are following a car driven by an elderly driver. You should

Mark one answer
- a   expect the driver to drive badly
- b   flash your lights and overtake
- c   be aware that the driver's reactions may not be as fast as yours
- d   stay close behind and drive carefully

Q194

A school crossing patrol shows this sign. What must you do?

Mark one answer

○ a   Continue if it is safe to do so
○ b   Slow down and be ready to stop
○ c   Stop ONLY if children are crossing
○ d   Stop at all times

Q195

You are approaching a school crossing patrol. When this sign is held up you must

Mark one answer

○ a   stop and allow any children to cross
○ b   stop and beckon the children to cross
○ c   stop only if the children are on a pedestrian crossing
○ d   stop only when the children are actually crossing the road

Q196

Where would you see this sign?

Mark one answer

○ a   In the window of a car taking children to school
○ b   At the side of the road
○ c   At playground areas
○ d   On the rear of a school bus or coach

Q197

You are parking your vehicle in the street. The car parked in front of you is displaying an orange badge. You should

Mark one answer

○ a   park close to it to save road space
○ b   allow room for a wheelchair
○ c   wait until the orange-badge holder returns
○ d   park with two wheels on the pavement

Driving Theory Test Questions

Q198

Where would you see this sign?

Mark one answer

- ○ a On the approach to a school crossing
- ○ b At a playground entrance
- ○ c On a school bus
- ○ d At a 'pedestrians only' area

Q199

You see a pedestrian with a white stick and two red reflective bands. This means that the person is

Mark one answer

- ○ a physically disabled
- ○ b deaf and dumb
- ○ c blind and dumb
- ○ d deaf and blind

Q200

You are following a motorcyclist on an uneven road. You should

Mark one answer

- ○ a allow less room to ensure that you can be seen in their mirrors
- ○ b overtake immediately
- ○ c allow extra room in case they swerve to avoid pot-holes
- ○ d allow the same room as normal because motorcyclists are not affected by road surfaces

Q201

What action would you take when elderly people are crossing the road?

Mark one answer

- ○ a Wave them across so they know that you've seen them
- ◉ b Be patient and allow them to cross in their own time
- ○ c Rev the engine to let them know that you're waiting
- ○ d Tap the horn in case they are hard of hearing

Q202

You should NEVER attempt to overtake a cyclist

Mark one answer

- ○ a just before you turn left
- ○ b just before you turn right
- ○ c on a one-way street
- ○ d on a dual carriageway

Q203

You are coming up to a roundabout. A cyclist is signalling to turn right. What should you do?

Mark one answer

- ○ a Overtake on the right
- ○ b Give a horn warning
- ○ c Signal the cyclist to move across
- ○ d Give the cyclist plenty of room

Q204

You are driving behind a cyclist. You wish to turn left just ahead. You should

Mark one answer

- a overtake the cyclist before the junction
- b pull alongside the cyclist and stay level until after the junction
- c hold back until the cyclist has passed the junction
- d go around the cyclist on the junction

Q205

You are driving behind two cyclists. They approach a roundabout in the left-hand lane. In which direction should you expect the cyclists to go?

Mark one answer

- a Left
- b Right
- c Any direction
- d Straight ahead

Q206

You are approaching this roundabout and see the cyclist signal right. Why is the cyclist keeping to the left?

Mark one answer

- a It is a quicker route for the cyclist
- b The cyclist is going to turn left instead
- c The cyclist thinks *The Highway Code* does not apply to bicycles
- d The cyclist is slower and more vulnerable

Q207

When you are overtaking a cyclist you should leave as much room as you would give to a car. Why is this?

Mark one answer

- a The cyclist might change lanes
- b The cyclist might get off the bike
- c The cyclist might swerve
- d The cyclist might have to make a right turn

Q208

You are waiting to come out of a side road. Why should you watch carefully for motorcycles?

Mark one answer

- a Motorcycles are usually faster than cars
- b Police patrols often use motorcycles
- c Motorcycles are small and hard to see
- d Motorcycles have right of way

Q209

Which TWO should you allow extra room when overtaking?

Mark two answers

- a Motorcycles
- b Tractors
- c Bicycles
- d Road-sweeping vehicles

Q210

Why should you allow extra room when overtaking a motorcyclist on a windy day?

Mark one answer

- a The rider may turn off suddenly to get out of the wind
- b The rider may be blown across in front of you
- c The rider may stop suddenly
- d The rider may be travelling faster than normal

Q211

Which of the following are hazards motorcyclists present in queues of traffic?

Mark three answers

- a Cutting in just in front of you
- b Riding in single file
- c Passing very close to your car
- d Riding with their headlamps on dipped beam
- e Filtering between the lanes

Q212

Which type of vehicle is most affected by strong winds?

Mark one answer

- a Tractor
- b Motorcycle
- c Car
- d Tanker

Q213

In daylight, an approaching motorcyclist is using a dipped headlight. Why?

Mark one answer

- a So that the rider can be seen more easily
- b To stop the battery over-charging
- c To improve the rider's vision
- d The rider is inviting you to proceed

Q214

Where should you take particular care to look out for motorcyclists and cyclists?

Mark one answer
- a On dual carriageways
- b At junctions
- c At zebra crossings
- d On one-way streets

Q215

Where in particular should you look out for motorcyclists?

Mark one answer
- a In a filling station
- b At a road junction
- c Near a service area
- d When entering a car park

Q216

At road junctions which of the following are most vulnerable?

Mark three answers
- a Cyclists
- b Motorcyclists
- c Pedestrians
- d Car drivers
- e Lorry drivers

Q217

Motorcyclists should wear bright clothing mainly because

Mark one answer
- a they must do so by law
- b it helps keep them cool in summer
- c the colours are popular
- d drivers often do not see them

Q218

Motorcycle riders are vulnerable because they

Mark one answer
- a are easy for other road users to see
- b are difficult for other road users to see
- c are likely to have breakdowns
- d cannot give arm signals

Q219

Motorcyclists ride in daylight with their headlights switched on because

Mark one answer
- a it is a legal requirement
- b there's a speed trap ahead
- c they need to be seen
- d there are speed humps ahead

Q220

There is a slow-moving motorcyclist ahead of you. You're unsure what the rider is going to do. You should

Mark one answer
- a pass on the left
- b pass on the right
- c stay behind
- d move closer

Q221

You are driving behind a moped. You want to turn left just ahead. You should

Mark one answer
- a overtake the moped before the junction
- b pull alongside the moped and stay level until just before the junction
- c sound your horn as a warning and pull in front of the moped
- d stay behind until the moped has passed the junction

Q222

Motorcyclists will often look round over their right shoulder just before turning right. This is because

Mark one answer
- a they need to listen for following traffic
- b motorcycles do not have mirrors
- c looking around helps them balance as they turn
- d they need to check for traffic in their blind area

Q223

When emerging from a side road into a queue of traffic which vehicles can be especially difficult to see?

Mark one answer
- a Motorcycles
- b Tractors
- c Milk floats
- d Cars

Q224

You want to turn right from a main road into a side road. Just before turning you should

Mark one answer
- a cancel your right-turn signal
- b select first gear
- c check for traffic overtaking on your right
- d stop and set the handbrake

Q225

You are driving on a main road. You intend to turn right into a side road. Just before turning you should

Mark one answer
- a adjust your interior mirror
- b flash your headlamps
- c steer over to the left
- d check for traffic overtaking on your offside

Q226

You are driving in slow-moving queues of traffic. Just before changing lane you should

Mark one answer
- a sound the horn
- b look for motorcyclists filtering through the traffic
- c give a 'slowing down' arm signal
- d change down to first gear

Q227

Which of the following are a major cause of motorcycle collisions?

Mark one answer

- a   Car drivers
- b   Moped riders
- c   Sunny weather conditions
- d   Traffic lights

Q228

You are driving in town. There's a bus at the bus stop on the other side of the road. Why should you be careful?

Mark one answer

- a   The bus may have broken down
- b   Pedestrians may come from behind the bus
- c   The bus may move off suddenly
- d   The bus may remain stationary

Q229

As you are driving along you meet a group of horses and riders from a riding school. Why should you be extra cautious?

Mark one answer

- a   They will be moving in single file
- b   They will be moving slowly
- c   Many of the riders may be learners
- d   The horses will panic more because they are in a group

Q230

Which THREE should you do when passing sheep on a road?

Mark three answers

- a   Allow plenty of room
- b   Drive very slowly
- c   Pass quickly but quietly
- d   Briefly sound your horn
- e   Be ready to stop

Q231

How should you overtake horse riders?

Mark one answer

- a   Drive up close and overtake as soon as possible
- b   Speed is not important but allow plenty of room
- c   Use your horn just once to warn them
- d   Drive slowly and leave plenty of room

Q232

You notice horse riders in front.
What should you do FIRST?

Mark one answer
- a   Pull out to the middle of the road
- b   Be prepared to slow down
- c   Accelerate around them
- d   Signal right

Q233

You are driving on a narrow country road.
Where would you find it most difficult to
see horses and riders ahead of you?

Mark one answer
- a   On left-hand bends
- b   When travelling downhill
- c   When travelling uphill
- d   On right-hand bends

Q234

A horse rider is in the left-hand lane
approaching a roundabout. The driver
behind should expect the rider to

Mark one answer
- a   go in any direction
- b   turn right
- c   turn left
- d   go ahead

Q235

Which age group is most likely to be
involved in a road accident?

Mark one answer
- a   36 to 45-year-olds
- b   55-year-olds and over
- c   46 to 55-year-olds
- d   17 to 25-year-olds

Q236

What's the most common factor in
causing road accidents?

Mark one answer
- a   Weather conditions
- b   Driver error
- c   Road conditions
- d   Mechanical failure

Q237

You have just passed your driving test.
How likely are you to have an accident,
compared with other drivers?

Mark one answer
- a   More likely
- b   It depends on your age
- c   Less likely
- d   About the same

Q238

As a new driver, how can you decrease
your risk of accidents on the motorway?

Mark one answer
- a   By keeping up with the car in front
- b   By never driving over 45 mph
- c   By driving only in the nearside lane
- d   By taking further training

Q239

How would you react to other drivers who appear to be inexperienced?

Mark one answer

- a Sound your horn to warn them of your presence
- b Be patient and prepared for them to react more slowly
- c Flash your headlights to indicate that it's safe for them to proceed
- d Overtake them as soon as possible

Q240

A friend wants to teach you to drive a car. They must

Mark one answer

- a be over 21 and have held a full licence for at least two years
- b be over 18 and hold an advanced driver's certificate
- c be over 18 and have fully comprehensive insurance
- d be over 21 and have held a full licence for at least three years

Q241

Your vehicle hits a pedestrian at 40 mph. The pedestrian will

Mark one answer

- a certainly be killed
- b certainly survive
- c probably be killed
- d probably survive

Q242

At night you see a pedestrian wearing reflective clothing and carrying a bright red light. What does this mean?

Mark one answer

- a You are approaching roadworks
- b You are approaching an organised march
- c You are approaching a slow-moving vehicle
- d You are approaching an accident black spot

Q243

A pedestrian steps out into the road just ahead of you. What should you do FIRST?

Mark one answer

- a Sound your horn
- b Check your mirror
- c Flash your headlights
- d Press the brake

Answers and Explanations

Q168 d Pedestrians are the most likely to expect as country roads often have no pavements and pedestrians are advised to walk on the right so that they can see oncoming traffic on their side of the road. However, you should always expect the unexpected when driving.

Q169 a Red triangles give warnings, in this case of people walking along the road. 'c' is a warning of a pedestrian crossing.

Q170 c

Q171 d When you turn into a side road pedestrians who are already crossing have priority so you must give way.

Q172 d

Q173 c

Q174 c

Q175 b

Q176 b

Q177 c

Q178 c You cannot turn right until you can see it is safe to do so. You should stop and then edge slowly forwards until you can see clearly to the left and right.

Q179 a, b, e

Q180 c

Q181 a, d You must never park on the zigzag lines. To be exact, you must not overtake the moving motor vehicle nearest the crossing or the leading vehicle which has stopped to give way to a pedestrian.

Q182 d

Q183 a, d

Q184 b You should never stop where you would block a pedestrian crossing except to prevent an accident.

Q185 d All are potential dangers but the child is the greatest risk.

Q186 d

Q187 c

Q188 b

Q189 d

Q190 d

Q191 c

Q192 d You must stop at a stop sign, in this case held by a school crossing patrol.

Q193 c

Q194 d

Q195 a

Q196 d

Q197 b

Q198 c

Q199 d

Q200 c

Q201 b

Q202 a The word 'NEVER' makes 'a' correct.

Q203 d

Q204 c As the question states you are turning left JUST ahead, you have no time to overtake the cyclist safely which is why 'c' is incorrect.

Q205 c Cyclists tend to keep to the left and you must always expect the unexpected.

Q206 d

Q207 c 'c' is the answer required, but you should also be aware that cyclists can be unpredictable.

Q208 c

Q209 a, c Motorcycles and bicycles can easily wobble off course and you need to allow them extra room.

Q210 b

Q211 a, c, e Check your door mirrors, especially before moving forwards or changing lanes.

Q212 b

Q213 a

Q214 b

Q215 b

Q216 a, b, c

Q217 d

Q218 b

Q219 c

Q220 c

Q221 d

Q222 d

Q223 a

Q224 c Use your right door mirror and look particularly for motorcyclists.

Q225 d

Q226 b

Q227 a

Q228 b

Q229 c The word 'extra' points to 'c' as the correct answer. In all situations you should be cautious when passing horses.

Q230 a, b, e

Q231 d

Q232 b Horses and their riders can be unpredictable so 'b' is the safest first action.

Q233 a While 'a' is correct, remember that narrow country roads often have banks, hedges, trees or other obstructions to your view as well

as bends, so sometimes 'd' might also be true.

Q234 a

Q235 d

Q236 b Statistics show that about 95% of accidents involve an element of human error.

Q237 a Your chances of having an accident are greatest in the first two years after passing your test regardless of your age.

Q238 d The other three possible answers are all potentially dangerous and 'd' is correct.

Q239 b

Q240 d

Q241 c When pedestrians are about 'kill your speed'.

Q242 b

Q243 d This is an emergency. What's happening in front of you is more important than what might happen behind you. Normally, try to anticipate these situations so that you can check your mirror first.

Driving Theory Test Questions

Other Vehicle Characteristics

Q244

The road is wet. Why might a motorcyclist steer around drain covers on a bend?

Mark one answer

- ○ a To avoid puncturing the tyres on the edge of the drain covers
- ◉ b To prevent the motorcycle sliding on the metal drain covers
- ○ c To help judge the bend using the drain covers as marker points
- ○ d To avoid splashing pedestrians on the pavement

Q245

It is very windy. You are behind a motorcyclist who is overtaking a high-sided vehicle. What should you do?

Mark one answer

- ○ a Overtake the motorcyclist immediately
- ◉ b Keep well back
- ○ c Stay level with the motorcyclist
- ○ d Keep close to the motorcyclist

Q246

Bells hanging high across the road surface are warning you

Mark one answer

- ○ a that you are approaching a high bridge
- ○ b of overhanging trees
- ○ c of overhead electrified cables
- ○ d that you are approaching a level crossing

Q247

It is very windy. You are about to overtake a motorcyclist. You should

Mark one answer

- ○ a overtake slowly
- ◉ b allow extra room
- ○ c sound your horn
- ○ d keep close as you pass

Q248

You are following a large articulated vehicle. It is going to turn left into a narrow road. What action should you take?

Mark one answer

- ○ a Move out and overtake on the offside
- ○ b Pass on the left as the vehicle moves out
- ◉ c Be prepared to stop behind
- ○ d Overtake quickly before the lorry moves out

Q249

You are following a long vehicle. It approaches a crossroads and signals left, but moves out to the right. You should

Mark one answer

- a   get closer in order to pass it quickly
- ◉ b   stay well back and give it room
- c   assume the signal's wrong and it's really turning right
- d   overtake as it starts to slow down

Q250

You are following a long vehicle approaching a crossroads. The driver signals right but moves close to the left-hand kerb. What should you do?

Mark one answer

- a   Warn the driver of the wrong signal
- ◉ b   Wait behind the long vehicle
- c   Report the driver to the police
- d   Overtake on the right-hand side

Q251

You are approaching a mini-roundabout. The long vehicle in front is signalling left but positioned over to the right. You should

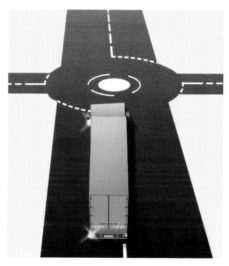

Mark one answer

- a   sound your horn
- b   overtake on the left
- c   follow the same course as the lorry
- ◉ d   keep well back

Q252

You are towing a caravan. Which is the safest type of rear view mirror to use?

Mark one answer

- a   Interior wide-angle-view mirror
- ◉ b   Extended-arm side mirrors
- c   Ordinary door mirrors
- d   Ordinary interior mirror

Q253

You keep well back while waiting to overtake a large vehicle. Another car fills the gap. You should

Mark one answer
- ○ a   sound your horn
- ○ b   drop back further
- ○ c   flash your headlights
- ○ d   start to overtake

Q254

Before overtaking a large vehicle you should keep well back. Why is this?

Mark one answer
- ○ a   To give acceleration space to overtake quickly on blind bends
- ○ b   To get the best view of the road ahead
- ○ c   To leave a gap in case the vehicle stops and rolls back
- ○ d   To offer other drivers a safe gap if they want to overtake you

Q255

You wish to overtake a long, slow-moving vehicle on a busy road. You should

Mark one answer
- ○ a   wait behind until the driver waves you past
- ○ b   flash your headlights for the oncoming traffic to give way
- ○ c   follow it closely and keep moving out to see the road ahead
- ○ d   keep well back until you can see that it is clear

Q256

You are driving downhill. There is a car parked on the other side of the road. Large, slow lorries are coming towards you. You should

Mark one answer
- ○ a   keep going because you have the right of way
- ○ b   slow down and give way
- ○ c   speed up and get past quickly
- ○ d   pull over on the right behind the parked car

Q257

When about to overtake a long vehicle you should

Mark one answer
- ○ a   sound the horn to warn the driver that you're there
- ○ b   stay well back from the lorry to obtain a better view
- ○ c   drive close to the lorry in order to pass more quickly
- ○ d   flash your lights and wait for the driver to signal when it is safe

Q258

The FIRST thing you should do when you want to overtake a large lorry is

Mark one answer
- ○ a   move close behind so that you can pass quickly
- ○ b   keep in close to the left-hand side
- ○ c   flash your headlights and wait for the driver to wave you on
- ○ d   stay well back to get a better view

Q259

Why is passing a lorry more risky than passing a car?

Mark one answer

- a   Lorries are longer than cars
- b   Lorries may suddenly pull up
- c   The brakes of lorries are not as good
- d   Lorries climb hills more slowly

Q260

You're driving along a road and you see this signal. It means

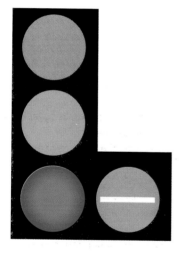

Mark one answer

- a   cars must stop
- b   trams must stop
- c   both trams and cars must stop
- d   both trams and cars can continue

Q261

You are travelling behind a bus that pulls up at a bus stop. What should you do?

Mark two answers

- a   Accelerate past the bus sounding your horn
- b   Watch carefully for pedestrians
- c   Be ready to give way to the bus
- d   Pull in closely behind the bus

Q262

When you approach a bus signalling to move off from a bus stop you should

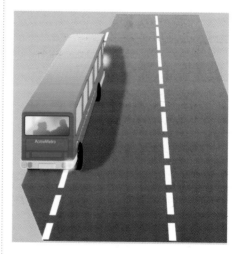

Mark one answer

- a   get past before it moves
- b   allow it to pull away, if it is safe to do so
- c   flash your headlamps as you approach
- d   signal left and wave the bus on

Q263

In which THREE places could a strong crosswind affect your course?

Mark three answers

○ a   After overtaking a large vehicle
○ b   When passing gaps in hedges
○ c   On exposed sections of roadway
○ d   In towns
○ e   In tunnels
○ f   When passing parked vehicles

Q264

You are following a large lorry on a wet road. Spray makes it difficult to see. You should

Mark one answer

○ a   drop back until you can see better
○ b   put your headlights on full beam
○ c   keep close to the lorry, away from the spray
○ d   speed up and overtake quickly

Q265

Which of these vehicles is LEAST likely to be affected by crosswinds?

Mark one answer

○ a   Cyclists
○ b   Motorcyclists
○ c   High-sided vehicles
○ d   Cars

Q266

What does 'tailgating' mean?

Mark one answer

○ a   When a vehicle delivering goods has its tailgate down
○ b   When a vehicle is travelling with its back doors open
○ c   When a driver is following another vehicle too closely
○ d   When stationary vehicles are too close in a queue

Q267

You are driving on a wet motorway with surface spray. You should

Mark one answer

○ a   use your hazard flashers
○ b   use dipped headlights
○ c   use your rear fog lights
○ d   drive in any lane with no traffic

Answers and Explanations

Q244 **b** Water on metal is a dangerous combination, especially for a two-wheeled vehicle.

Q245 **b** Let the motorcyclist complete the overtake before even thinking about following.

Q246 **c**

Q247 **b** Motorcycles may have problems with strong crosswinds.

Q248 **c** The large articulated vehicle may need to position to the right in order to turn left into the narrow road.

Q249 **b**

Q250 **b** Long vehicles require more space to turn and often need to position for this.

Q251 **d**

Q252 **b**

Q253 **b**

Q254 **b** You cannot see ahead if you are too close to a large vehicle in front of you.

Q255 **d**

Q256 **b**

Q257 **b**

Q258 **d** This allows you the visibility and space to plan the overtaking manoeuvre.

Q259 **a** Overtaking takes time, so the longer the vehicle you overtake the greater the danger as you will take longer to pass it.

Q260 **b**

Q261 **b, c**

Q262 **b** This helps traffic flow without giving confusing signals

Q263 **a, b, c**

Q264 **a**

Q265 **d** Of the four mentioned, cars are by far the most stable and least affected by crosswinds.

Q266 **c**

Q267 **b** Spray reduces visibility. You should use dipped headlights when visibility is reduced.

Driving Theory Test Questions

Own Vehicle Handling

Q268

You should not drive with your foot on the clutch for longer than necessary because it

Mark one answer

- a   increases wear on the gearbox
- b   increases petrol consumption
- ◑ c   reduces your control of the vehicle
- d   reduces the grip of the tyres

Q269

What are TWO main reasons why coasting downhill is wrong?

Mark two answers

- a   Petrol consumption will be higher
- ◑ b   The vehicle will pick up speed
- c   It puts more wear and tear on the tyres
- d   You have less braking and steering control
- e   It damages the engine

Q270

You are following a vehicle at a safe distance on a wet road. Another driver overtakes you and pulls into the gap you have left. What should you do?

Mark one answer

- a   Flash your headlights as a warning
- b   Try to overtake safely as soon as you can
- c   Drop back to regain a safe distance
- d   Stay close to the other vehicle until it moves on

Q271

Why is coasting wrong?

Mark one answer

- a   It will cause the car to skid
- b   It will make the engine stall
- c   The engine will run faster
- d   There is no engine braking

Q272

Which THREE of the following will affect your stopping distance?

Mark three answers

- a   How fast you are going
- b   The tyres on your vehicle
- c   The time of day
- d   The weather
- e   The street lighting

Q273

You are approaching a bend at speed. You should begin to brake

Mark one answer

- a   on the bend
- b   after the bend
- c   after changing gears
- d   before the bend

Q274

You should avoid 'coasting' your vehicle because it could

Mark one answer

- a   damage the suspension
- b   increase tyre wear
- c   flatten the battery
- d   reduce steering control

Q275

Why is pressing the clutch down for long periods a bad habit?

Mark one answer

- a It reduces the car's speed when going downhill
- b It causes the engine to wear out more quickly
- c It reduces the driver's control of the vehicle
- d It causes the engine to use more fuel

Q276

You are driving in the left-hand lane of a dual carriageway. Another vehicle overtakes and pulls in front of you leaving you without enough separation distance. You should

Mark one answer

- a move to the right lane
- b continue as you are
- c drop back
- d sound your horn

Q277

You are driving on the motorway in windy conditions. When passing high-sided vehicles you should

Mark one answer

- a increase your speed
- b be wary of a sudden gust
- c drive alongside very closely
- d expect normal conditions

Q278

You wish to overtake on a dual carriageway. You see in your mirror that the car behind has pulled out to overtake you. You should

Mark one answer

- a not signal until the car has passed
- b signal and pull out to overtake
- c signal to tell the driver behind that you also want to overtake
- d touch the brakes to show your brake lights

Q279

How should you drive around a bend on ice?

Mark one answer

- a Using the clutch and brake together
- b In first gear
- c Braking as you enter the bend
- d Slowly and smoothly

Q280

Give two reasons for using an additive in the windscreen washer reservoir.

Mark two answers

- a To prevent freezing in winter
- b To wipe off leaves in autumn
- c To help prevent mould growth
- d To clear dead insects in summer
- e To prevent corrosion

Q281

In which THREE of these situations may you overtake another vehicle on the left?

Mark three answers

- a When you are in a one-way street
- b When approaching a motorway slip road where you will be turning off
- c When the vehicle in front is signalling to turn right
- d When a slower vehicle is travelling in the right-hand lane of a dual carriageway
- e In slow-moving traffic queues when traffic in the right-hand lane is moving more slowly

Q282

When snow is falling heavily you should

Mark one answer

- a drive as long as your headlights are used
- b not drive unless you have a mobile phone
- c drive only when your journey is short
- d not drive unless it's essential

Q283

You are driving on an icy road. What distance should you drive from the car in front?

Mark one answer

- a Eight times the normal distance
- b Six times the normal distance
- c Ten times the normal distance
- d Four times the normal distance

Q284

How can you best control your vehicle when driving in snow?

Mark one answer

- a By driving slowly in as high a gear as possible
- b By staying in low gear and gripping the steering wheel tightly
- c By driving in first gear
- d By keeping the engine revs high and slipping the clutch

Q285

You have to make a journey in foggy conditions. You should

Mark one answer

- a follow closely other vehicles' tail lights
- b never use demisters and windscreen wipers
- c leave plenty of time for your journey
- d keep two seconds behind other vehicles

Q286

To correct a rear-wheel skid you should

Mark one answer

- a not turn at all
- b turn away from it
- c turn into it
- d apply your handbrake

Q287

Why should you test your brakes after this hazard?

Ford

Mark one answer
- a Because you will be driving on a slippery road
- b Because your brakes will be soaking wet
- c Because you will have driven down a long hill
- d Because you will have just crossed a long bridge

Q288

You are driving in very wet weather. Your vehicle begins to slide. This effect is called

Mark one answer
- a hosing
- b weaving
- c aquaplaning
- d fading

Q289

You should switch your rear fog lights on when visibility drops below

Mark one answer
- a your overall stopping distance
- b ten car lengths
- c 10 metres (33 feet)
- d 100 metres (330 feet)

Q290

You have to make a journey in fog. What are the TWO most important things you should do before you set out?

Mark two answers
- a Top up the radiator with antifreeze
- b Make sure that you have a warning triangle in the vehicle
- c Check that your lights are working
- d Check the battery
- e Make sure that the windows are clean

Q291

You are following other vehicles in fog with your lights on. How else can you reduce the chances of being involved in an accident?

Mark one answer
- a Keep close to the vehicle in front
- b Use your main beam instead of dipped headlights
- c Keep together with the faster vehicles
- d Reduce your speed and increase the gap

Q292

You should only use rear fog lights when you cannot see further than about

Mark one answer
- a 100 metres (330 feet)
- b 200 metres (660 feet)
- c 250 metres (800 feet)
- d 150 metres (495 feet)

Q293

Why should you always reduce your speed when driving in fog?

Mark one answer

○ a Because the brakes do not work as well

○ b Because you could be dazzled by other people's fog lights

○ c Because the engine's colder

● d Because it is more difficult to see events ahead

Q294

You are overtaking a car at night. You must be sure that

Mark one answer

○ a you flash your headlamps before overtaking

○ b your rear fog lights are switched on

○ c you have switched your lights to full beam before overtaking

○ d you do not dazzle other road users

Q295

Which TWO of the following are correct? When overtaking at night you should

Mark two answers

○ a wait until a bend so that you can see the oncoming headlights

○ b sound your horn twice before moving out

○ c be careful because you can see less

○ d beware of bends in the road ahead

○ e put headlights on full beam

Q296

You are driving in fog. The car behind seems to be very close. You should

Mark one answer

○ a switch on your hazard warning lights

○ b pull over and stop immediately

○ c speed up to get away

○ d continue cautiously

Q297

Which TWO are correct? The passing places on a single-track road are

Mark two answers

○ a for taking a rest from driving

○ b to pull into if an oncoming vehicle wants to proceed

○ c for stopping and checking your route

○ d to turn the car around in, if you are lost

○ e to pull into if the car behind wants to overtake

Q298

You are driving in fog. Why should you keep well back from the vehicle in front?

Mark one answer

○ a In case it changes direction suddenly

○ b In case its fog lights dazzle you

○ c In case it stops suddenly

○ d In case its brake lights dazzle you

Q299

You are driving in poor visibility. You can see more than 100 metres (330 feet) ahead. How can you make sure that other drivers can see you?

Mark one answer
- a Turn on your dipped headlights
- b Follow the vehicle in front closely
- c Turn on your rear fog lights
- d Keep well out towards the middle of the road

Q300

You are driving on a motorway in fog. The left-hand edge of the motorway can be identified by reflective studs. What colour are they?

Mark one answer
- a Green
- b Amber
- c Red
- d White

Q301

While driving, the fog clears and you can see more clearly. You must remember to

Mark one answer
- a switch off the fog lights
- b reduce your speed
- c switch off the demister
- d close any open windows

Q302

You have to park on the road in fog. You should

Mark one answer
- a leave sidelights on
- b leave dipped headlights and fog lights on
- c leave dipped headlights on
- d leave main beam headlights on

Q303

On a foggy day you unavoidably have to park your car on the road. You should

Mark one answer
- a leave your headlights on
- b leave your fog lights on
- c leave your sidelights on
- d leave your hazard lights on

Q304

You are driving on a well-lit motorway at night. You must

Mark one answer
- a use only your sidelights
- b always use your headlights
- c always use rear fog lights
- d use headlights only in bad weather

Q305

When driving towards a bright setting sun, glare can be reduced by

Mark one answer
- a closing one eye
- b dipping the interior mirror
- c wearing dark glasses
- d looking sideways

Q306

You are driving on a motorway at night. You MUST have your headlights switched on unless

Mark one answer

○ a   there are vehicles close in front of you
○ b   you are travelling below 50 mph
○ c   the motorway is lit
○ d   your vehicle is broken down on the hard shoulder

Q307

You are on a narrow road at night. A slower-moving vehicle ahead has been signalling right for some time. What should you do?

Mark one answer

○ a   Overtake on the left
○ b   Flash your headlights before overtaking
● c   Signal right and sound your horn
○ d   Wait for the signal to be cancelled before overtaking

Q308

You are driving at night. Why should you be extra careful of your speed?

Mark one answer

○ a   Because you might need to stop within the distance that you can see
○ b   Because it uses more petrol
○ c   Because driving with the lights on runs down the battery
○ d   Because you may be late

Q309

You are travelling on a motorway at night with other vehicles just ahead of you. Which lights should you have on?

Mark one answer

○ a   Front fog lights
○ b   Main beam headlights
○ c   Sidelights only
○ d   Dipped headlights

Q310

You are travelling at night. You are dazzled by headlights coming towards you. You should

Mark one answer

○ a   pull down your sun visor
○ b   slow down or stop
○ c   switch on your main beam headlights
○ d   put your hand over your eyes

Q311

You are dazzled by oncoming headlights when driving at night. What should you do?

Mark one answer

○ a   Slow down or stop
○ b   Brake hard
○ c   Drive faster past the oncoming car
○ d   Flash your lights

Q312

A rumble device is designed to

Mark two answers

- ○ a give directions
- ○ b prevent cattle escaping
- ○ c alert drivers to low tyre pressure
- ○ d alert drivers to a hazard
- ○ e encourage drivers to reduce speed

Q313

You see a vehicle coming towards you on a single-track road. You should

Mark one answer

- ○ a stop at a passing place
- ○ b reverse back to the main road
- ○ c do an emergency stop
- ○ d put on your hazard flashers

Answers and Explanations

Q268 c Driving with the clutch down ('coasting') reduces control.

Q269 b, d

Q270 c This may feel irritating, particularly if the circumstance is repeated several times. However, it is safest and, in reality, causes no delay.

Q271 d You are coasting when you push down the clutch, disconnecting both engine and gear box.

Q272 a, b, d

Q273 d Avoid braking on a bend. You risk losing the control of your vehicle. Get the speed right before the bend, accelerate gently through the bend and then get the car back up to speed.

Q274 d

Q275 c With the clutch down you separate the engine from the road wheels. You cannot, for example, accelerate out of danger.

Q276 c You need to adjust your separation distance continually. Don't get annoyed by this – it keeps you safe and does not add to your journey time.

Q277 b

Q278 a If you signal as described in 'c' you may confuse the driver behind who may assume you intend to pull out immediately, so 'a' is safest.

Q279 d The more gentle your movements on ice, the less likely you are to skid. You need as high a gear as possible, gentle use of the accelerator, a low speed and as little use of the brakes as possible.

Q280 a, d

Q281 a, c, e

Q282 d

Q283 c Stopping distances can be up to ten times longer in snow and ice. Give yourself plenty of time to stop.

Q284 a This gives a greater safety margin and avoids wheel spin.

Q285 c *The Highway Code* advises you to allow more time for your journey in foggy conditions. However, always ask yourself if the journey really is necessary.

Q286 c This answer refers to steering. For example, if the back of your car skids to the right, you should turn the wheel carefully to the right to correct it.

Q287 **b** After driving through water your brakes will be wet, and wet brakes are inefficient.

Q288 **c** Surface water builds up a film between the road and the tyres, causing the car to drive on the film of water and not grip the road surface. The steering will feel very light if you are aquaplaning. Release the gas pedal.

Q289 **d** Remember to switch them off when the visibility improves.

Q290 **c, e** See and be seen are the two most crucial safety aspects of driving in fog.

Q291 **d**

Q292 **a**

Q293 **d** Everybody knows this but an alarming number of people don't put the knowledge into practice. Accidents happen as a result.

Q294 **d** You may need to switch to full-beam headlights as you overtake, but not before.

Q295 **c, d** 'c' and 'd' are the correct answers. 'a' and 'b' are dangerous, but be aware that as you overtake 'c' may be necessary, particularly if the vehicle you overtake dips its headlights as you overtake it.

Q296 **d**

Q297 **b, e**

Q298 **c** If the car in front stops suddenly you may run into it if you have been driving too close. If it changes direction left or right it will have no effect on you.

Q299 **a** This is the safest way to be seen. 'b' is obviously dangerous. 'c' is illegal as visibility is more than 100 metres, and anyway only helps drivers behind. 'd' could cause an accident if an oncoming driver has the same idea.

Q300 **c** Red reflective studs separate the left-hand lane and the hard shoulder.

Q301 **a** Fog lights should only be used where visibility is down to about 100 metres. Otherwise you risk dazzling other drivers.

Q302 **a**

Q303 **c**

Q304 **b**

Q305 **c**

Q306 **d** You must use your headlights on motorways at nights even if the motorway is lit.

Q307 **d**

Q308 **a**

Q309 **d** Full-beam headlights would dazzle the drivers in front by reflecting in their mirrors.

Q310 **b**

Q311 **a**

Q312 **d, e** (NB: a rumble device is normally raised strips or markings on the surface of the road.)

Q313 **a** Bear in mind that single-track roads may have passing places at long intervals. You may meet an oncoming vehicle at a point where one of you will need to reverse to the previous nearest passing point.

Driving Theory Test Questions

Roads and Regulations – Motorways

Q314

The left-hand lane on a three-lane motorway is for use by

Mark one answer

- a   any vehicle
- b   large vehicles only
- c   emergency vehicles only
- d   slow vehicles only

Q315

Which of the following CAN travel on a motorway?

Mark one answer

- a   Cyclists
- b   Vans
- c   Farm tractors
- d   Learner drivers

Q316

Which FOUR of these must not use motorways?

Mark four answers

- a   Learner car drivers
- b   Motorcycles over 50cc
- c   Double-decker buses
- d   Farm tractors
- e   Horse riders
- f   Cyclists

Q317

As a provisional licence-holder you should not drive a car

Mark one answer

- a   over 50 mph
- b   at night
- c   on the motorway
- d   with passengers in rear seats

Q318

What is the national speed limit for cars and motorcycles in the centre lane of a three-lane motorway?

Mark one answer

- a   40 mph
- b   50 mph
- c   60 mph
- d   70 mph

Q319

What is the national speed limit on motorways for cars and motorcycles?

Mark one answer

- a   30 mph
- b   50 mph
- c   60 mph
- d   70 mph

Q320

You are towing a trailer on a motorway. What is your maximum speed limit?

Mark one answer

- a   40 mph
- b   50 mph
- c   60 mph
- d   70 mph

Q321

Why is it particularly important to carry out a check on your vehicle before making a long motorway journey?

Mark one answer

○ a You will have to do more harsh braking on motorways
○ b Motorway service stations do not deal with breakdowns
○ c The road surface will wear down the tyres faster
○ d Continuous high speeds may increase the risk of your vehicle breaking down

Q322

Immediately after joining a motorway you should normally

Mark one answer

○ a try to overtake
○ b readjust your mirrors
○ c position your vehicle in the centre lane
○ d keep in the left lane

Q323

You are joining a motorway. Why is it important to make full use of the slip road?

Mark one answer

○ a Because there is space available to reverse if you need to
○ b To allow you direct access to the overtaking lanes
○ c To build up a speed similar to traffic on the motorway
○ d Because you can continue on the hard shoulder

Q324

You are joining a motorway from a slip road on the left. You should

Mark one answer

○ a adjust your speed to the speed of the traffic on the motorway
○ b accelerate as quickly as you can and drive straight out
○ c drive onto the hard shoulder until a gap appears
○ d give a left signal to join the motorway

Q325

When joining a motorway you must always

Mark one answer

○ a use the hard shoulder
○ b stop at the end of the acceleration lane
○ c come to a stop before joining the motorway
○ d give way to traffic already on the motorway

Q326

You are driving a car on a motorway. Unless signs show otherwise you must NOT exceed

Mark one answer

○ a 50 mph
○ b 60 mph
○ c 70 mph
○ d 80 mph

Q327

Which of the these IS NOT allowed to travel in the right-hand lane of a three-lane motorway?

Mark one answer

- a   A small delivery van
- b   A motorcycle
- c   A vehicle towing a trailer
- d   A motorcycle and side-car

Q328

On motorways you should never overtake on the left UNLESS

Mark one answer

- a   you can see well ahead that the hard shoulder is clear
- b   the traffic in the right-hand lane is signalling right
- c   you warn drivers behind by signalling left
- d   there is a queue of traffic to your right that is moving more slowly

Q329

A basic rule when driving on motorways is

Mark one answer

- a   use the lane that has least traffic
- b   keep to the left lane unless overtaking
- c   overtake on the side that is clearest
- d   try to keep above 50 mph to prevent congestion

Q330

The left-hand lane of a motorway should be used for

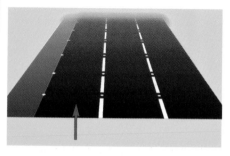

Mark one answer

- a   breakdowns and emergencies only
- b   overtaking slower traffic in the other lanes
- c   slow vehicles only
- d   normal driving

Q331

On a three-lane motorway which lane should you use for normal driving?

Mark one answer

- a   Left
- b   Right
- c   Centre
- d   Either the right or centre

Q332

You are driving on a three-lane motorway at 70 mph. There is no traffic ahead. Which lane should you use?

Mark one answer

- a   Any lane
- b   Middle lane
- c   Right lane
- d   Left lane

Q333

You are driving on a motorway. You have to slow down quickly due to a hazard. You should

Mark one answer
- a switch on your hazard lights
- b switch on your headlights
- c sound your horn
- d flash your headlights

Q334

You are driving on a motorway. The car ahead shows its hazard lights for a short time. This tells you that

Mark one answer
- a the driver wants you to overtake
- b the other car is going to change lanes
- c traffic ahead is slowing or stopping suddenly
- d there is a police speed check up ahead

Q335

You get a puncture on the motorway. You manage to get your vehicle onto the hard shoulder. You should

Mark one answer
- a change the wheel yourself immediately
- b use the emergency telephone and call for assistance
- c try to wave down another vehicle for help
- d only change the wheel if you have a passenger to help you

Q336

Which vehicles are normally fitted with amber flashing beacons on the roof?

Mark two answers
- a Doctor's car
- b Bomb disposal team
- c Blood transfusion team
- d Breakdown recovery vehicles
- e Coastguard
- f Maintenance vehicles

Q337

What is the right-hand lane used for on a three-lane motorway?

Mark one answer
- a Emergency vehicles only
- b Overtaking
- c Vehicles towing trailers
- d Coaches only

Q338

For what reason may you use the right-hand lane of a motorway

Mark one answer
- a To keep out of the way of lorries
- b For driving at more than 70 mph
- c For turning right
- d For overtaking other vehicles

Q339

How should you use the emergency telephone on a motorway?

Mark one answer
- a Stay close to the carriageway
- b Face the oncoming traffic
- c Keep your back to the traffic
- d Keep your head in the kiosk

Q340

On a motorway you may ONLY stop on the hard shoulder

Mark one answer

- a   in an emergency
- b   if you feel tired and need to rest
- c   if you accidentally go past the exit that you wanted to take
- d   to pick up a hitchhiker

Q341

You are driving on a motorway. You have to slow down quickly due to a hazard. You should

Mark one answer

- a   switch on your headlights
- b   switch on your hazard lights
- c   sound your horn
- d   flash your headlights

Q342

What should you use the hard shoulder of a motorway for?

Mark one answer

- a   Stopping in an emergency
- b   Overtaking
- c   Stopping when you are tired
- d   Joining the motorway

Q343

After a breakdown you need to rejoin the main carriageway of a motorway from the hard shoulder. You should

Mark one answer

- a   move out onto the carriageway then build up your speed
- b   move out onto the carriageway using your hazard lights
- c   gain speed on the hard shoulder before moving out onto the carriageway
- d   wait on the hard shoulder until someone flashes their headlights at you

Q344

The minimum safe time gap to keep between you and the vehicle in front in good conditions is at least

Mark one answer

- a   four seconds
- b   one second
- c   three seconds
- d   two seconds

Q345

Your vehicle has broken down on a motorway. You are not able to stop on the hard shoulder. What should you do FIRST?

Mark one answer

- a Switch on your hazard warning lights
- b Stop following traffic and ask for help
- c Attempt to repair your vehicle quickly
- d Place a warning triangle in the road

Q346

You are travelling in the left-hand lane of a busy motorway. Signs indicate that your lane is closed 800 yards ahead. You should

Mark one answer

- a signal right, then pull up and wait for someone to give way
- b switch on your hazard warning lights and edge over to the lane on your right
- c wait until you reach the obstruction, then move across to the right
- d move over to the lane on your right as soon as it is safe to do so

Q347

What colour are the reflective studs between a motorway and its slip road?

Mark one answer

- a Amber
- b White
- c Green
- d Red

Q348

When may you stop on a motorway?

Mark three answers

- a If you have to read a map
- b When you are tired and need a rest
- c If red lights show above your lane
- d When told to by the police
- e If a child in the car feels ill
- f In an emergency or a breakdown

Q349

You are driving on a motorway. There are red flashing lights above your lane. You must

Mark one answer

- a pull onto the hard shoulder
- b slow down and watch for further signals
- c leave at the next exit
- d stop and wait

Q350

You are travelling on a motorway. What colour are the reflective studs on the left of the carriageway?

Mark one answer
- a   Green
- b   Red
- c   White
- d   Amber

Q351

When driving through a contraflow system on a motorway you should

Mark one answer
- a   ensure that you do not exceed 30 mph, for safety
- b   keep a good distance from the vehicle ahead, for safety
- c   switch lanes to keep the traffic flowing
- d   drive close to the vehicle ahead to reduce queues

Q352

You are intending to leave the motorway at the next exit. Before you reach the exit you should normally position your vehicle

Mark one answer
- a   in the middle lane
- b   in the left-hand lane
- c   on the hard shoulder
- d   in any lane

Q353

What do these motorway signs show?

Mark one answer
- a   They are countdown markers to a bridge
- b   They are distance markers to the next telephone
- c   They are countdown markers to the next exit
- d   They warn of a police control ahead

Q354

You are driving on a three-lane motorway. There are red reflective studs on your left and white ones to your right. Where are you?

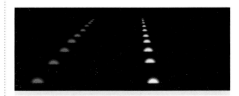

Mark one answer
- a   In the right-hand lane
- b   In the middle lane
- c   On the hard shoulder
- d   In the left-hand lane

Q355

At night, when leaving a well-lit motorway service area, you should

Mark one answer

- a drive for some time using only your sidelights
- b give your eyes time to adjust to the darkness
- c switch on your interior light until your eyes adjust
- d close your eyes for a moment before leaving the slip road

Q356

You are driving on a motorway. By mistake, you go past the exit that you wanted to take. You should

Mark one answer

- a carefully reverse on the hard shoulder
- b carry on to the next exit
- c carefully reverse in the left-hand lane
- d make a U-turn at the next gap in the central reservation

Q357

On a motorway the reflective amber studs can be found between

Mark one answer

- a the hard shoulder and the carriageway
- b the acceleration lane and the carriageway
- c the central reservation and the carriageway
- d each pair of the lanes

Answers and Explanations

Q314 **a** Strictly speaking, any vehicle which is allowed on a motorway.

Q315 **b**

Q316 **a, d, e, f**

Q317 **c**

Q318 **d**

Q319 **d** The national speed limit for cars and motorcycles is 70 mph on motorways and dual carriageways and 60 mph on single-lane roads.

Q320 **c** Remember that when towing a trailer strong winds can affect stability.

Q321 **d** You should check oil and windscreen washer levels and also check the tyres. Plan your rest stops.

Q322 **d**

Q323 **c** You need to build up your speed to that of the traffic already on the motorway so that you can ease into a gap in the flow of traffic.

Q324 **a** Use your mirrors and look over your shoulder quickly to judge a safe gap to merge into. Remember that you should give way to traffic already on the motorway. Try to avoid stopping at the end of the acceleration lane.

Q325 **d**

Q326 **c**

Q327 **c**

Q328 **d**

Q329 **b**

Q330 **d**

Q331 **a** The other lanes should be used for overtaking.

Q332 **d** You should always use the left-hand lane for normal driving.

Q333 a

Q334 c

Q335 b Whenever you break down make sure you use your warning triangle, and keep as far from the carriageway as possible.

Q336 d, f

Q337 b

Q338 d

Q339 b

Q340 a

Q341 b

Q342 a You may only stop on the hard shoulder in an emergency.

Q343 c

Q344 d In distance, this gives you one metre per mph of speed. Therefore at 70 mph, using the two-second rule, you would be leaving a gap of 70 metres.

Q345 a Note that this is your FIRST action.

Q346 d Always look well ahead, which will give plenty of time to change lanes safely.

Q347 c

Q348 c, d, f Do remember that motorway service areas are not officially part of the motorway.

Q349 d

Q350 b

Q351 b In these circumstances there may also be a speed limit – keep to it.

Q352 b

Q353 c They are 100 metres (330 feet) apart.

Q354 d Red reflective studs mark the join between the left-hand lane and the hard shoulder. White reflective studs mark the lanes.

Q355 b

Q356 b You can never reverse on a motorway.

Q357 c

Driving Theory Test Questions

Roads and Regulations – Other Roads

Q358

What is the meaning of this sign?

Mark one answer

- a   Local speed limit applies
- b   No waiting on the carriageway
- c   National speed limit applies
- d   No entry to vehicular traffic

Q359

What is the national speed limit for cars and motorcycles on a dual carriageway?

Mark one answer

- a   30 mph
- b   50 mph
- c   60 mph
- d   70 mph

Q360

A single carriageway road has this sign. What's the maximum permitted speed for a car towing a trailer?

Mark one answer

- a   30 mph
- b   40 mph
- c   50 mph
- d   60 mph

Q361

What is the national speed limit on a single carriageway road for cars and motorcycles?

Mark one answer

- a   70 mph
- b   60 mph
- c   50 mph
- d   30 mph

Q362

You are driving along a road that has no traffic signs. There are street lights. What is the speed limit?

Mark one answer

- a   20 mph
- b   30 mph
- c   40 mph
- d   60 mph

Q363

There are no speed limit signs on the road. How is a 30 mph limit indicated?

Mark one answer

- a   By hazard warning lines
- b   By street lighting
- c   By pedestrian islands
- d   By double or single yellow lines

Q364

Where you see street lights but no speed limit signs the limit is usually

Mark one answer

- a   30 mph
- b   40 mph
- c   50 mph
- d   60 mph

Q365

You see this sign ahead of you. It means

Mark one answer

- a start to slow down to 30 mph after passing it
- b you are leaving the 30 mph speed limit area
- c do not exceed 30 mph after passing it
- d the minimum speed limit ahead is 30 mph

Q366

If you see a 30 mph limit ahead it means

Mark one answer

- a that the restriction applies only during the working day
- b that you must not exceed this speed
- c that it is a guide and you are allowed to drive 10% faster
- d that you must keep your speed up to 30 mph

Q367

What does a speed limit sign like this mean?

Mark one answer

- a It is safe to drive at the speed shown
- b The speed shown is the advised maximum
- c The speed shown allows for various road and weather conditions
- d You must not exceed the speed shown

Q368

You are towing a small caravan on a dual carriageway. You must not exceed

Mark one answer

- a 50 mph
- b 40 mph
- c 70 mph
- d 60 mph

Q369

What does this sign mean?

Mark one answer
- a   Minimum speed 30 mph
- b   End of maximum speed
- c   End of minimum speed
- d   Maximum speed 30 mph

Q370

You are driving along a street with parked vehicles on the left-hand side. For which THREE reasons must you keep your speed down?

Mark three answers
- a   So that oncoming traffic can see you more clearly
- b   You may set off car alarms
- c   Vehicles may be pulling out
- d   Drivers' doors may open
- e   Children may run out from between the vehicles

Q371

You meet an obstruction on your side of the road. You must

Mark one answer
- a   drive on; it is your right of way
- b   give way to oncoming traffic
- c   wave oncoming vehicles through
- d   accelerate to get past first

Q372

There is a tractor ahead of you. You wish to overtake but you are NOT sure if it is safe to do so. You should

Mark one answer
- a   follow another overtaking vehicle through
- b   sound your horn to the slow vehicle to pull over
- c   speed through but flash your lights to oncoming traffic
- d   not overtake if you are in doubt

Q373

You are leaving your vehicle parked on a road. When may you leave the engine running?

Mark one answer
- a   If you will be parked for less than five minutes
- b   If the battery is flat
- c   If there is a passenger in the vehicle
- d   Not on any occasion

Q374

In which FOUR places must you NOT park or wait?

Mark four answers
- a   On a dual carriageway
- b   At a bus stop
- c   On the slope of a hill.
- d   Opposite a traffic island
- e   In front of someone else's drive
- f   On the brow of a hill

Q375

What is the nearest you may park your vehicle to a junction?

Mark one answer
- ○ a 10 metres (33 feet)
- ○ b 12 metres (40 feet)
- ○ c 15 metres (50 feet)
- ○ d 20 metres (65 feet)

Q376

In which TWO places must you NOT park?

Mark two answers
- ○ a Near a school entrance
- ○ b Near a police station
- ○ c In a side road
- ○ d At a bus stop
- ○ e In a one-way street

Q377

In which THREE places must you NEVER park your vehicle?

Mark three answers
- ○ a Near the brow of a hill
- ○ b At or near a bus stop
- ○ c Where there is no pavement
- ○ d Within 10 metres (33 feet) of a junction
- ○ e On a 40 mph road

Q378

You want to park and you see this sign. On the days and times shown you should

Mark one answer
- ○ a park in a bay and not pay
- ○ b park on yellow lines and pay
- ○ c park on yellow lines and not pay
- ○ d park in a bay and pay

Q379

What is the meaning of this sign?

Mark one answer
- ○ a No entry
- ○ b Waiting restrictions
- ○ c National speed limit
- ○ d School crossing patrol

Q380

At which of these places are you sometimes allowed to park your vehicle?

Mark one answer

- a   On the nearside lane of a motorway
- b   On a clearway
- c   Where there is a single broken yellow line
- d   On the zigzag lines of a zebra crossing

Q381

What MUST you have to park in a disabled space?

Mark one answer

- a   An orange badge
- b   A wheelchair
- c   An advanced driver certificate
- d   A modified vehicle

Q382

You are looking for somewhere to park your vehicle. The area is full EXCEPT for spaces marked 'disabled use'. You must

Mark one answer

- a   use these spaces when elsewhere is full
- b   stay with your vehicle when you park there
- c   use these spaces, disabled or not
- d   not park there unless permitted

Q383

Your vehicle is parked on the road at night. When must you use sidelights?

Mark one answer

- a   Where there are continuous white lines in the middle of the road
- b   Where the speed limit exceeds 30 mph
- c   Where you are facing oncoming traffic
- d   Where you are near a bus stop

Q384

You park overnight on a road with a 40 mph speed limit. You should

Mark one answer

- a   park facing the traffic
- b   park with sidelights on
- c   park with dipped headlights on
- d   park near a street light

Q385

On a three-lane dual carriageway the right-hand lane can be used for

Mark one answer
- ○ a   overtaking only, never turning right
- ○ b   overtaking or turning right
- ○ c   fast-moving traffic only
- ○ d   turning right only, never overtaking

Q386

You are driving in the right lane of a dual carriageway. You see signs showing that the right lane is closed 800 yards ahead. You should

GET IN LANE

800 yards

Mark one answer
- ○ a   keep in that lane until you reach the queue
- ○ b   move to the left immediately
- ○ c   wait and see which lane is moving faster
- ○ d   move to the left in good time

Q387

You can park on the right-hand side of a road at night

Mark one answer
- ○ a   in a one-way street
- ○ b   with your sidelights on
- ○ c   more than 10 metres (33 feet) from a junction
- ○ d   under a lamp-post

Q388

You are driving at night with full beam headlights on. A vehicle is overtaking you. You should dip your lights

Mark one answer
- ○ a   some time after the vehicle has passed you
- ○ b   before the vehicle starts to pass you
- ○ c   only if the other driver dips his headlights
- ○ d   as soon as the vehicle passes you

Q389

You are driving on a two-lane dual carriageway. For which TWO of the following would you use the right-hand lane?

Mark two answers
- ○ a   Turning right
- ○ b   Normal driving
- ○ c   Driving at the minimum allowed speed
- ○ d   Constant high-speed driving
- ○ e   Overtaking slower traffic
- ○ f   Mending punctures

Q390

You are entering an area of roadworks. There is a temporary speed limit displayed. You must

Mark one answer

- a not exceed the speed limit
- b obey the limit only during rush hour
- c accept the speed limit as advisable
- d obey the limit except for overnight

Q391

While driving, you approach roadworks. You see a temporary maximum speed limit sign. You must

Mark one answer

- a comply with the sign during the working day
- b comply with the sign at all times
- c comply with the sign when the lanes are narrow
- d comply with the sign during the hours of darkness

Q392

As a car driver which THREE lanes must you NOT use?

Mark three answers

- a Crawler lane
- b Bus lane at the times shown
- c Overtaking lane
- d Acceleration lane
- e Cycle lane
- f Tram lane

Q393

You may drive a motor car in this bus lane

Mark one answer

- a outside its operation hours
- b to get to the front of a traffic queue
- c at no times at all
- d to overtake slow-moving traffic

Q394

You are driving on a road that has a cycle lane. The lane is marked by a solid white line. This means that

Mark two answers

- a you must not drive in the lane unless it is unavoidable
- b the lane cannot be used for parking your vehicle
- c you can drive in the lane at any time
- d the lane must be used by motorcyclists in heavy traffic

Q395

You are approaching a busy junction. There are several lanes with road markings. At the last moment you realise that you are in the wrong lane. You should

Mark one answer

- a   continue in that lane
- b   force your way across
- c   stop until the area has cleared
- d   use clear arm signals to cut across

Q396

Where may you overtake on a one-way street?

Mark one answer

- a   Only on the left-hand side
- b   Overtaking is not allowed
- c   Only on the right-hand side
- d   Either on the right or the left

Q397

You are going along a single-track road with passing places only on the right. The driver behind wishes to overtake. You should

Mark one answer

- a   speed up to get away from the following driver
- b   switch on your hazard warning lights
- c   wait opposite a passing place on your right
- d   drive into a passing place on your right

Q398

You are on a road that is only wide enough for one vehicle. There is a car coming towards you. Which TWO of these would be correct?

Mark two answers

- a   Pull into a passing place on your right
- b   Force the other driver to reverse
- c   Pull into a passing place if your vehicle is wider
- d   Pull into a passing place on your left
- e   Wait opposite a passing place on your right
- f   Wait opposite a passing place on your left

Q399

Signals are normally given by direction indicators and

Mark one answer

- a   brake lights
- b   side lights
- c   fog lights
- d   interior lights

Q400

When going straight ahead at a roundabout you should

Mark one answer

- a   indicate left before leaving the roundabout
- b   not indicate at any time
- c   indicate right when approaching the roundabout
- d   indicate left when approaching the roundabout

Q401

Which vehicle might have to use a different course to normal at roundabouts?

Mark one answer
- ○ a   Sports car
- ○ b   Van
- ○ c   Estate car
- ○ d   Long vehicle

Q402

You are going straight ahead at a roundabout. How should you signal?

Mark one answer
- ⦿ a   Signal right on the approach and then left to leave the roundabout
- ○ b   Signal left as you leave the roundabout
- ○ c   Signal left on the approach to the roundabout and keep the signal on until you leave
- ○ d   Signal left just after you pass the exit before the one you'll take

Q403

While driving, you intend to turn left into a minor road. On the approach you should

Mark one answer
- ○ a   keep just left of the middle of the road
- ○ b   keep in the middle of the road
- ○ c   swing out wide just before turning
- ⦿ d   keep well to the left of the road

Q404

You may make a U-turn

Mark one answer
- ○ a   when it is safe on a wide road
- ○ b   on a motorway, when it is safe
- ○ c   in a wide one-way street
- ○ d   by mounting both pavements carefully

Q405

At a crossroads there are no signs or road markings. Two vehicles approach. Which has priority?

Mark one answer
- ○ a   Neither vehicle
- ○ b   The vehicle travelling the fastest
- ○ c   The vehicle on the widest road
- ○ d   Vehicles approaching from the right

Q406

At a crossroads with no road markings who has priority?

Mark one answer
- ○ a   Traffic from the left
- ○ b   Traffic from the right
- ○ c   Nobody
- ○ d   Traffic from ahead

Q407

Who has priority at an unmarked crossroads?

Mark one answer
- ○ a   The driver of the larger vehicle
- ○ b   No one
- ○ c   The driver who is going faster
- ○ d   The driver on the wider road

Q408

You are intending to turn right at a junction. An oncoming driver is also turning right. It will normally be safer to

Mark one answer

- a keep the other vehicle to your RIGHT and turn behind it (offside to offside)
- b keep the other vehicle to your LEFT and turn in front of it (nearside to nearside)
- c carry on and turn at the next junction instead
- d hold back and wait for the other driver to turn first

Q409

You may only enter a box junction when

Mark one answer

- a there are less than two vehicles in front of you
- b the traffic lights show green
- c your exit road is clear
- d you need to turn left

Q410

You may wait in a yellow box junction when

Mark one answer

- a oncoming traffic is preventing you from turning right
- b you are in a queue of traffic turning left
- c you are in a queue of traffic to go ahead
- d you are on a roundabout

Q411

You want to turn right at a box junction. You should

Mark one answer

- a wait in the box junction until your exit is clear
- b wait before the junction until it is clear of all traffic
- c drive on; you cannot turn right at a box junction
- d drive slowly into the box junction when signalled by oncoming traffic

Q412

On which THREE occasions MUST you stop your vehicle?

Mark three answers

- a When involved in an accident
- b At a red traffic light
- c When signalled to do so by a police officer
- d At a junction with double broken white lines
- e At a pelican crossing when the amber light is flashing and no pedestrians are crossing

Q413

You MUST stop when signalled to do so by which THREE of these?

Mark three answers

- ⊘ a   A police officer
- ◯ b   A pedestrian
- ⊗ c   A school crossing patrol
- ◯ d   A bus driver
- ⊘ e   A red traffic light

Q414

You are waiting at a level crossing. The red warning lights continue to flash after a train has passed by. What should you do?

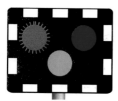

Mark one answer

- ◯ a   Get out and investigate
- ◯ b   Telephone the signal operator
- ⊘ c   Continue to wait
- ◯ d   Drive across carefully

Q415

You are waiting at a level crossing. A train has passed but the lights keep flashing. You must

Mark one answer

- ◯ a   carry on waiting
- ◯ b   phone the signal operator
- ◯ c   edge over the stop line and look for trains
- ◯ d   park your vehicle and investigate

Q416

You are driving over a level crossing. The warning lights come on and a bell rings. What should you do?

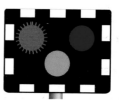

Mark one answer

- ◯ a   Get everyone out of the vehicle immediately
- ◯ b   Stop and reverse back to clear the crossing
- ⊗ c   Keep going and clear the crossing
- ◯ d   Stop immediately and use your hazard warning lights

Q417

You will see these markers when approaching

Mark one answer

- ◯ a   a concealed level crossing
- ◯ b   the end of a motorway
- ◯ c   a concealed 'road narrows' sign
- ◯ d   the end of a dual carriageway

Q418

At toucan crossings, apart from pedestrians you should be aware of

Mark one answer

- a   emergency vehicles emerging
- b   buses pulling out
- c   trams crossing in front
- d   cyclists riding across

Q419

Who can use a toucan crossing?

Mark two answers

- a   Trains
- b   Cyclists
- c   Buses
- d   Pedestrians
- e   Trams

Q420

At a pelican crossing, what does a flashing amber light mean?

Mark one answer

- a   You must not move off until the lights stop flashing
- b   You must give way to pedestrians still on the crossing
- c   You can move off, even if pedestrians are still on the crossing
- d   You must stop because the lights are about to change to red

Q421

You are on a busy main road and find that you are travelling in the wrong direction. What should you do?

Mark one answer

- a   Turn into a side road on the right and reverse into the main road
- b   Make a U-turn in the main road
- c   Make a 'three-point' turn in the main road
- d   Turn round in a side road

Q422

You may drive on a footpath

Mark one answer

- a   to overtake slow-moving traffic
- b   when the pavement is very wide
- c   if no pedestrians are near
- d   to get into a property

Q423

You are parked in a busy high street. What is the safest way to turn your vehicle around to go the opposite way?

Mark one answer

- a   Find a quiet side road to turn round in
- b   Drive into a side road and reverse into the main road
- c   Get someone to stop the traffic
- d   Do a U-turn

Q424

You may remove your seat belt when carrying out a manoeuvre that involves

Mark one answer
- a   reversing
- b   a hill start
- c   an emergency stop
- d   driving slowly

Q425

You must not reverse

Mark one answer
- a   for longer than necessary
- b   for more than a car's length
- c   into a side road
- d   in a built-up area

Q426

When you're NOT sure that it's safe to reverse your vehicle you should

Mark one answer
- a   use your horn
- b   rev your engine
- c   get out and check
- d   reverse slowly

Q427

When may you reverse from a side road into a main road?

Mark one answer
- a   Only if both roads are clear of traffic
- b   Not at any time
- c   At any time
- d   Only if the main road is clear of traffic

Q428

You are reversing your vehicle into a side road. When would the greatest hazard to passing traffic occur?

Mark one answer
- a   After you have completed the manoeuvre
- b   Just before you actually begin to manoeuvre
- c   After you have entered the side road
- d   When the front of your vehicle swings out

Answers and Explanations

Q358 c
Q359 d The national speed limit is 70 mph on a motorway or dual carriageway and 60 mph on two-way roads unless traffic signs denote anything different.
Q360 c
Q361 b
Q362 b If there are street lights, the speed limit is 30 mph unless a road sign states otherwise.
Q363 b
Q364 a If there is any difference there would be repeated signs on the light posts.
Q365 c You should adjust your speed so that you are travelling at no more than 30 mph as you pass the sign.
Q366 b
Q367 d This sign gives an order which tells you the maximum speed at which you are allowed to drive. It is a law, not a piece of advice, and does not in any way imply that it will always be safe to drive at that speed.
Q368 d
Q369 c
Q370 c, d, e
Q371 b
Q372 d
Q373 d
Q374 b, d, e, f
Q375 a
Q376 a, d
Q377 a, b, d
Q378 d
Q379 b

Q380 c You are NEVER allowed to park at 'a', 'b' or 'd'.
Q381 a
Q382 d
Q383 b You are not allowed to park at 'a' or 'd' at any time; 'c' is wrong because you must park on the left at night unless in a one-way street.
Q384 b
Q385 b
Q386 d 'b' is incorrect because it may not be safe to move to the left immediately.
Q387 a
Q388 d If you dip your lights too early you may reduce your vision; too late and you may dazzle the driver who has overtaken.
Q389 a, e
Q390 a
Q391 b
Q392 b, e, f
Q393 a
Q394 a, b
Q395 a All the other actions suggested could be dangerous.
Q396 d In a one-way street you are allowed to overtake on either side, provided it is safe.
Q397 c
Q398 d, e
Q399 a When you press your brake pedal the brake lights come on, warning other vehicles behind.
Q400 a You should signal left just as you pass the exit before the one you want to take.
Q401 d
Q402 d This is correct for most

roundabouts. Bear in mind that some roundabouts do not have an exit to the left, so the first exit is straight ahead.

Q403 **d**

Q404 **a**

Q405 **a** You often find these on housing estates. Approach with caution and be prepared to give way.

Q406 **c**

Q407 **b** An unmarked crossroads has no road signs or road markings and no vehicle has priority even if one road is wider or busier than the other.

Q408 **a** You can see the oncoming traffic more easily from this position.

Q409 **c**

Q410 **a**

Q411 **a**

Q412 **a, b, c** 'd' is wrong because although the double, broken white lines at a junction mean 'give way', you do not necessarily have to stop in order to do so. 'e' is wrong because you may drive on at a pelican crossing when the amber light is flashing if no pedestrians are crossing.

Q413 **a, c, e** Note the word 'MUST' in the question, which is asking what the law says.

Q414 **c** You should wait for three minutes. If no further train passes you should telephone the signal operator.

Q415 **a**

Q416 **c** You are already on the crossing when the warning lights come on,

so 'c' is correct.

Q417 **a** These countdown markers indicate the distance to the stop line at the concealed level crossing.

Q418 **d** Cyclists are allowed to ride across toucan crossings, unlike other crossings where they must dismount.

Q419 **b, d** Toucan crossings are shared by pedestrians and cyclists together.

Q420 **b** You may drive as soon as the crossing is clear and before the flashing amber light changes to green.

Q421 **d** It is illegal to reverse from a minor to a major road, so 'a' is wrong. 'b' and 'c' would be dangerous because the road is busy.

Q422 **d**

Q423 **a**

Q424 **a**

Q425 **a**

Q426 **c**

Q427 **b**

Q428 **d** Always remember to check all round just before steering and give way to any road users.

Driving Theory Test Questions

Signs and Signals

Q429

You MUST obey signs giving orders.
These signs are mostly in

Mark one answer
- a — green rectangles
- b red triangles
- c blue rectangles
- d red circles

Q430

Traffic signs giving orders are generally
which shape?

Mark one answer

- a
- b

- c
- d

Q431

Which type of sign tells you NOT
to do something?

Mark one answer

- a
- b

- c
- d

Q432

What does this sign mean?

Mark one answer
- a Maximum speed limit with traffic calming
- b Minimum speed limit with traffic calming
- c '20 cars only' parking zone
- d Only 20 cars allowed at any one time

Q433

Which sign means no motor vehicles are allowed?

Mark one answer

 a

 b

 c

 d

Q434

What does this sign mean?

Mark one answer
- a New speed limit 20 mph
- b No vehicles over 30 tonnes
- c Minimum speed limit 30 mph
- d End of 20 mph zone

Q435

What does this sign mean?

Mark one answer
- a No overtaking
- b No motor vehicles
- c Clearway (no stopping)
- d Cars and motorcycles only

Q436

What does this sign mean?

Mark one answer
- a No parking
- b No road markings
- c No through road
- d No entry

Q437

What does this sign mean?

Mark one answer

- a Bend to the right
- b Road on the right closed
- c No traffic from the right
- d No right turn

Q438

Which sign means 'no entry'?

Mark one answer

a

b

c

d

Q439

What does this sign mean?

Mark one answer

- a Route for trams only
- b Route for buses only
- c Parking for buses only
- d Parking for trams only

Q440

Which type of vehicle does this sign apply to?

Mark one answer

- a Wide vehicles
- b Long vehicles
- c High vehicles
- d Heavy vehicles

Q441

Which sign means NO motor vehicles allowed?

Mark one answer

○ a

○ b

○ c

○ d

Q442

What does this sign mean?

Mark one answer

○ a   Do not overtake.
○ b   Oncoming cars have priority
○ c   Two-way traffic
○ d   No right turn ahead

Q443

Which sign means no overtaking?

Mark one answer

○ a

○ b

○ c

○ d

Q444

What does this sign mean?

Mark one answer

○ a   Waiting restrictions apply
○ b   Waiting permitted
○ c   National speed limit applies
○ d   Clearway (no stopping)

Q445

What does this sign mean?

Mark one answer
- a You have priority
- b No motor vehicles
- c Two-way traffic
- d No overtaking

Q446

What does this sign mean?

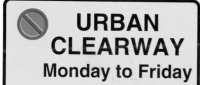

Mark one answer
- a You can park on the days and times shown
- b No parking on the days and times shown
- c No parking at all from Monday to Friday
- d You can park at any time: the urban clearway ends

Q447

What does this sign mean?

Mark one answer
- a End of restricted speed area
- b End of restricted parking area
- c End of clearway
- d End of cycle route

Q448

Which sign means 'no stopping'?

Mark one answer

- a

- b

- c

- d

Q449

What does this sign mean?

Mark one answer

- a Roundabout
- b Crossroads
- c No stopping
- d No entry

Q450

What does this sign mean?

Mark one answer

- a Keep in one lane
- b Priority to traffic coming towards you
- c Do not overtake
- d Form two lanes

Q451

What does this sign mean?

Mark one answer

- a Distance to parking place ahead
- b Distance to public telephone ahead
- c Distance to public house ahead
- d Distance to passing place ahead

Q452

What does this sign mean?

Mark one answer

- a Vehicles may not park on the verge or footway
- b Vehicles may park on the left-hand side of the road only
- c Vehicles may park fully on the verge or footway
- d Vehicles may park on the right-hand side of the road only

Q453

You see this sign ahead. It means

Mark one answer

- a national speed limit applies
- b waiting restrictions apply
- c no stopping
- d no entry

Q454

What does this traffic sign mean?

Mark one answer

- a No overtaking allowed
- b Give priority to oncoming traffic
- c No U-turns allowed
- d One-way traffic only

Q455

What is the meaning of this traffic sign?

Mark one answer

- a End of two-way road
- b Give priority to vehicles coming towards you
- c You have priority over vehicles coming towards you
- d Bus lane ahead

Q456

What should you do when you see this sign?

Mark one answer

- a Stop, ONLY if traffic is approaching
- b Stop, even if the road is clear
- c Stop, ONLY if children are waiting to cross
- d Stop, ONLY if a red light is showing

Q457

What shape is a stop sign at a junction?

Mark one answer

○ a

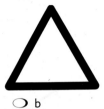
○ b

○ c

◐ d

Q458

Which shape of traffic sign means that you must stop?

Mark one answer

○ a

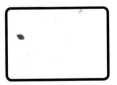
○ b

◐ c

○ d

Q459

Which sign means 'traffic has priority over oncoming vehicles'?

Mark one answer

○ a

○ b

◐ c

○ d

Q460

What does this sign mean?

Mark one answer
○ a   Service area 30 miles ahead
○ b   Maximum speed 30 mph
◐ c   Minimum speed 30 mph
○ d   Lay-by 30 miles ahead

Q461

What does this sign mean?

Mark one answer

- a No overtaking
- b You are entering a one-way street
- c Two-way traffic ahead
- ● d You have priority over vehicles from the opposite direction

Q462

At a mini-roundabout you should

Mark one answer

- a give way to traffic from the right
- b give way to traffic from the left
- c give way to traffic from the other way
- d stop even when empty

Q463

What does this sign mean?

Mark one answer

- a Give way to oncoming vehicles
- b Approaching traffic passes you on both sides
- c Turn off at the next available junction
- d Pass either side to get to the same destination

Q464

What does this sign mean?

Mark one answer

- a Route for trams
- b Give way to trams
- c Route for buses
- d Give way to buses

Q465

What does a circular traffic sign with a blue background do?

Mark one answer

○ a   Give warning of a motorway ahead
○ b   Give directions to a car park
○ c   Give motorway information
○ d   Give an instruction

Q466

Which of these signs means that you are entering a one-way street?

Mark one answer

○ a

○ b

○ c

○ d

Q467

Where would you see a contraflow bus and cycle lane?

Mark one answer

○ a   On a dual carriageway
○ b   On a roundabout
○ c   On an urban motorway
○ d   On a one-way street

Q468

What does this sign mean?

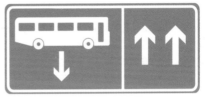

Mark one answer

○ a   Bus station on the right
○ b   Contraflow bus lane
○ c   With-flow bus lane
○ d   Give way to buses

Q469

What does this sign mean

Mark one answer

○ a   With-flow bus and cycle lane
○ b   Contraflow bus and cycle lane
○ c   No buses and cycles allowed
○ d   No waiting for buses and cycles

Q470

What does a sign with a brown background show?

Mark one answer

- a Tourist directions
- b Primary roads
- c Motorway routes
- d Minor routes

Q471

What are triangular signs for?

Mark one answer

- a To give warnings
- b To give information
- c To give orders
- d To give directions

Q472

What does this sign mean?

Mark one answer

- a Turn left ahead
- b T-junction
- c No through road
- d Give way

Q473

What does this sign mean?

Mark one answer

- a Crossroads
- b Level crossing with gate
- c Level crossing without gate
- d Ahead only

Q474

What does this sign mean?

Mark one answer

- a Ring road
- b Mini-roundabout
- c Restriction ends
- d Roundabout

Q475

Which FOUR of these would be indicated by a triangular road sign?

Mark four answers
- ⦵ a Road narrows
- ◯ b Ahead only
- ⦵ c Low bridge
- ◯ d Minimum speed
- ◯ e Children crossing
- ⦵ f T-junction

Q476

What does this sign mean?

Mark one answer
- ◯ a Cyclists must dismount
- ◯ b Bicycles are not allowed
- ◯ c You are approaching a cycle route
- ◯ d Walking is not allowed

Q477

What does this sign mean?

Mark one answer
- ◯ a No footpath ahead
- ◯ b Pedestrians only ahead
- ⦵ c Pedestrian crossing ahead
- ◯ d School crossing ahead

Q478

Which of these signs means there is a double bend ahead?

Mark one answer

◯ a   ◯ b

◯ c   ◯ d

Q479

What does this sign mean?

Mark one answer

- a   School crossing patrol
- b   No pedestrians allowed
- c   Pedestrian zone – no vehicles
- d   Pedestrian crossing ahead

Q480

What does this sign mean?

Mark one answer

- a   Wait at the barriers
- b   Wait at the crossroads
- c   Give way to trams
- d   Give way to farm vehicles

Q481

What does this sign mean?

Mark one answer

- a   Humpback bridge
- b   Humps in the road
- c   Entrance to tunnel
- d   Steep hill upwards

Q482

What does this sign mean?

Mark one answer

- a   Low bridge ahead
- b   Tunnel ahead
- c   Ancient monument ahead
- d   Accident black spot ahead

Q483

What does this sign mean?

Mark one answer

- a Two-way traffic ahead
- b Two-way traffic crossing a one-way street
- c Two-way traffic over a bridge
- d Two-way traffic crosses a two-way road

Q484

Which sign means 'two-way traffic crosses a one-way road'?

Mark one answer

a

b

c

d

Q485

Which of these signs means the end of a dual carriageway?

Mark one answer

a

b

c

d

Q486

What does this sign mean?

Mark one answer

- a End of dual carriageway
- b Tall bridge
- c Road narrows
- d End of narrow bridge

Q487

What does this sign mean?

Mark one answer

- a   Two-way traffic ahead across a one-way street
- b   Traffic approaching you has priority
- c   Two-way traffic straight ahead
- d   Motorway contraflow system ahead

Q488

What does this sign mean?

Mark one answer

- a   Crosswinds
- b   Road noise
- c   Airport
- d   Adverse camber

Q489

What does this traffic sign mean?

Mark one answer

- a   Slippery road ahead
- b   Tyres liable to punctures ahead
- c   Danger ahead
- d   Service area ahead

Q490

What does this sign mean?

Mark one answer

- a   Quayside or river bank
- b   Steep hill downwards
- c   Slippery road
- d   Road liable to flooding

Q491

What does this sign mean?

Mark one answer

- ○ a   Uneven road surface
- ○ b   Bridge over the road
- ○ c   Road ahead ends
- ○ d   Water across the road

Q492

What does this sign mean?

Mark one answer

- ○ a   Humpback bridge
- ○ b   Traffic calming hump
- ○ c   Low bridge
- ○ d   Uneven road

Q493

What does this sign mean?

Mark one answer

- ○ a   Turn left for parking area
- ○ b   No through road on the left
- ○ c   No entry for traffic turning left
- ○ d   Turn left for ferry terminal

Q494

Which sign means 'no through road'?

Mark one answer

○ a

○ b

○ c

○ d

Q495

You are about to overtake when you see this sign. You should

Mark one answer

- a overtake the other driver as quickly as possible
- b move right to get a better view
- c switch your headlights on before overtaking
- d hold back until you can see clearly ahead

Q496

Which is the sign for a ring road?

Mark one answer

- a

- b

- c

- d

Q497

What does this sign mean?

Mark one answer

- a Hilly road
- b Humps in road
- c Holiday route
- d Hospital route

Q498

What does this sign mean?

Mark one answer

- a The right-hand lane ahead is narrow
- b Right-hand lane for buses only
- c No turning to the right
- d The right-hand lane is closed

Q499

What does this sign mean?

Mark one answer
- a Change to the left lane
- b Leave at the next exit
- c Contraflow system
- d One-way street

Q500

You see this traffic light ahead. Which light(s) will come on next?

Mark one answer
- a Red alone
- b Red and amber together
- c Green and amber together
- d Green alone

Q501

You are approaching a red traffic light. The signal will change from red to

Mark one answer
- a red and amber, then green
- b green, then amber
- c amber, then green
- d green and amber, then green

Q502

A red traffic light means

Mark one answer
- a you should stop unless turning left
- b stop, if you are able to brake safely
- c you must stop and wait behind the stop line
- d proceed with caution

Q503

At traffic lights, amber on its own means

Mark one answer
- a prepare to go
- b go if the way is clear
- c go if no pedestrians are crossing
- d stop at the stop line

Q504

A red traffic light means

Mark one answer
- a you must stop behind the white stop line
- b you may drive straight on if there is no other traffic
- c you may turn left if it is safe to do so
- d you must slow down and prepare to stop if traffic has started to cross

Q505

You are approaching traffic lights. Red and amber are showing. This means

Mark one answer
- a pass the lights if the road is clear
- b there is a fault with the lights – take care
- c wait for the green light before you pass the lights
- d the lights are about to change to red

Q506

What does this sign mean?

Mark one answer
- a Route for lorries
- b Ring road
- c Rest area
- d Roundabout

Q507

You are at a junction controlled by traffic lights. When should you NOT proceed at green?

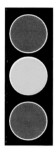

Mark one answer

- a When pedestrians are waiting to cross
- b When your exit from the junction is blocked
- c When you think the lights may be about to change
- d When you intend to turn right

Q508

What does this sign mean?

Mark one answer

- a Traffic lights out of order
- b Amber signal out of order
- c Temporary traffic lights ahead
- d New traffic lights ahead

Q509

What does this sign mean?

Mark one answer

- a Railway station
- b Route for cyclists
- c Ring road
- d Scenic route

Q510

You are in the left-hand lane at traffic lights. You are waiting to turn left. At which of these traffic lights must you NOT move on?

Mark one answer

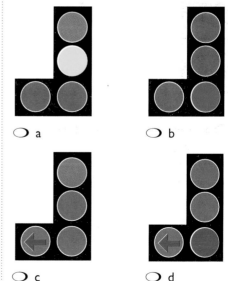

a   b

c   d

Q511

When traffic lights are out of order, who has priority?

Mark one answer

- a   Traffic going straight on
- b   Traffic turning right
- c   Nobody
- d   Traffic turning left

Q512

These flashing red lights mean STOP. In which THREE of the following places could you find them?

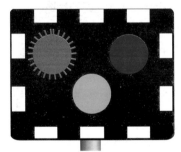

Mark three answers

- a   Pelican crossings
- b   Lifting bridges
- c   Zebra crossings
- d   Level crossings
- e   Motorway exits
- f   Fire stations

Q513

What do these zigzag lines at pedestrian crossings mean?

Mark one answer

- a   No parking at any time
- b   Parking allowed only for a short time
- c   Slow down to 20 mph
- d   Sounding horns is not allowed

Q514

A white line like this along the centre of the road is a

Mark one answer

- a   bus lane marking
- b   hazard warning
- c   'give way' marking
- d   lane marking

Q515

You are approaching a zebra crossing where pedestrians are waiting. Which arm signal might you give?

Mark one answer

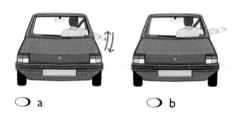

○ a   ○ b

○ c   ○ d

Q516

When may you cross a double solid white line in the middle of the road?

Mark one answer

○ a   To pass traffic that is queuing back at a junction

○ b   To pass a car signalling to turn left ahead

○ c   To pass a road maintenance vehicle travelling at 10 mph or less

○ d   To pass a vehicle that is towing a trailer

Q517

What does this road marking mean?

Mark one answer

○ a   Do not cross the line

○ b   No stopping allowed

○ c   You are approaching a hazard

○ d   No overtaking allowed

Q518

Where would you see this road marking?

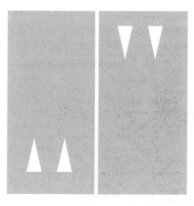

Mark one answer

○ a   At traffic lights

○ b   On road humps

○ c   Near a level crossing

○ d   At a box junction

Q519

Which is a hazard warning line?

Mark one answer

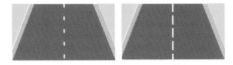

◯ a   ◯ b

◯ c   ◯ d

Q520

What does this sign mean?

Mark one answer

◯ a   Leave motorway at next exit
◯ b   Lane for heavy and slow vehicles
◯ c   All lorries use the hard shoulder
◯ d   Rest area for lorries

Q521

At this junction there is a stop sign with a solid white line on the road surface. Why is there a stop sign here?

Mark one answer

◯ a   Speed on the major road is de-restricted
◯ b   It is a busy junction
◯ c   Visibility along the major road is restricted
◯ d   There are hazard warning lines in the centre of the road

Q522

You see this line across the road at the entrance to a roundabout. What does it mean?

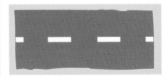

Mark one answer

◯ a   Give way to traffic from the right
◯ b   Traffic from the left has right of way
◯ c   You have right of way
◯ d   Stop at the line

Q523

Where would you find this road marking?

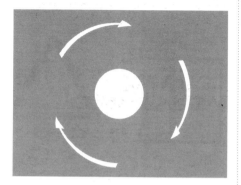

Mark one answer

- a   At a railway crossing
- b   At a junction
- c   On a motorway
- d   On a pedestrian crossing

Q524

You approach a junction. The traffic lights are not working. A police officer gives this signal. You should

Mark one answer

- a   turn left only
- b   turn right only
- c   stop level with the officer's arm
- d   stop at the stop line

Q525

How will a police officer in a patrol vehicle get you to stop?

Mark one answer

- a   Flash the headlights, indicate left and point to the left
- b   Wait until you stop, then approach you
- c   Use the siren, overtake, cut in front and stop
- d   Pull alongside you, use the siren and wave you to stop

Q526

There is a police car following you. The police officer flashes the headlights and points to the left. What should you do?

Mark one answer

- a   Turn at the next left
- b   Pull up on the left
- c   Stop immediately
- d   Move over to the left

Q527

The driver of the car in front is giving this arm signal. What does it mean?

Mark one answer

- a   The driver is slowing down
- b   The driver intends to turn right
- c   The driver wishes to overtake
- ● d   The driver intends to turn left

Q528

The driver of this car is giving a hand signal. What is he about to do?

Mark one answer
- a   Turn to the left
- b   Turn to the right
- c   Go straight ahead
- d   Let pedestrians cross

Q529

Your indicators are difficult to see due to bright sunshine. When using them you should

Mark one answer
- a   also give an arm signal
- b   sound your horn
- c   flash your headlights
- d   keep both hands on the steering wheel

Q530

You want to turn right at a junction but you think that your indicators cannot be seen clearly. What should you do?

Mark one answer
- a   Get out and check if your indicators can be seen
- b   Stay in the left-hand lane
- c   Keep well over to the right
- d   Give an arm signal as well as an indicator signal

Q531

Which arm signal tells a following vehicle that you intend to turn left?

Mark one answer

- a

- b

- c

- d

Q532

When may you sound the horn on your vehicle?

Mark one answer
- a   To give you right of way
- b   To attract a friend's attention
- c   To warn other drivers of your presence
- d   To make slower drivers move over

Signs and Signals

Q533

When motorists flash their headlights at you it means

Mark one answer

- a   that there is a radar speed trap ahead
- b   that they are giving way to you
- c   that they are warning you of their presence
- d   that there is something wrong with your vehicle

Q534

Where would you see these road markings?

Mark one answer

- a   At a level crossing
- b   On a motorway slip road
- c   At a pedestrian crossing
- d   On a single-track road

Q535

You are waiting at a T-junction. A vehicle is coming from the right with the left signal flashing. What should you do?

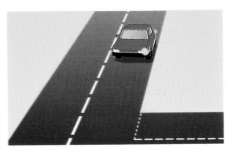

Mark one answer

- a   Move out and accelerate hard
- b   Wait until the vehicle starts to turn in
- c   Pull out before the vehicle reaches the junction
- d   Move out slowly

Q536

When may you use hazard warning lights when driving?

Mark one answer

- a   Instead of sounding the horn in a built-up area between 11.30 pm and 7 am
- b   On a motorway, or unrestricted dual carriageway, to warn of a hazard ahead
- c   On rural routes, after a warning sign of animals
- d   On the approach to toucan crossings, where cyclists are waiting to cross

Q537

Why should you make sure that you have cancelled your indicators after turning?

Mark one answer

- a   To avoid flattening the battery
- b   To avoid misleading other road users
- c   To avoid dazzling other road users
- d   To avoid damage to the indicator relay

Q538

When may you NOT overtake on the left?

Mark one answer

- a   On a free-flowing motorway or dual carriageway
- b   When the traffic is moving slowly in queues
- c   On a one-way street
- d   When the car in front is signalling to turn right

Q539

What does this motorway sign mean?

Mark one answer

- a   Change to the lane on your left
- b   Leave the motorway at the next exit
- c   Change to the opposite carriageway
- d   Pull up on the hard shoulder

Q540

You are driving on a motorway. There is a slow-moving vehicle ahead. On the back you see this sign. You should

Mark one answer

- a   pass on the right
- b   pass on the left
- c   leave at the next exit
- d   drive no further

Q541

What does this motorway sign mean?

Mark one answer

- a   Temporary minimum speed 50 mph
- b   No services for 50 miles
- c   Obstruction 50 metres (165 feet) ahead
- d   Temporary maximum speed 50 mph

Q542

What does this sign mean?

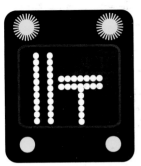

Mark one answer

- a   Through traffic to use left lane
- b   Right-hand lane T-junction only
- c   Right-hand lane closed ahead
- d   II tonne weight limit

Q543

On a motorway this sign means

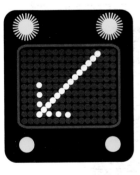

Mark one answer

- a   move over onto the hard shoulder
- b   pass a temporary obstruction on the left
- c   leave the motorway at the next exit
- d   move to the lane on your left

Q544

What does '25' mean on this motorway sign?

Mark one answer

- a   The distance to the nearest town
- b   The route number of the road
- c   The number of the next junction
- d   The speed limit on the slip road

Q545

Where can you find reflective amber studs on a motorway?

Mark one answer

- a   Separating the slip road from the motorway
- b   On the left-hand edge of the road
- c   On the right-hand edge of the road
- d   Separating the lanes

Q546

The right-hand lane of a three-lane motorway is

Mark one answer

- a   for lorries only
- b   an overtaking lane
- c   the right-turn lane
- d   an acceleration lane

Q547

You are driving on a motorway. Red flashing lights appear above your lane. What should you do?

Mark one answer

- a   Continue in that lane and await further information
- b   Go no further in that lane
- c   Drive onto the hard shoulder
- d   Stop and wait for an instruction to proceed

Q548

Where on a motorway would you find green reflective studs?

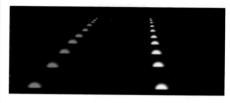

Mark one answer

- a   Separating driving lanes
- b   Between the hard shoulder and the carriageway
- c   At slip road entrances and exits
- d   Between the carriageway and the central reservation

Q549

You are travelling along a motorway. You see this sign. You should

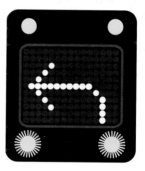

Mark one answer

- a   leave the motorway at the next exit
- b   turn left immediately
- c   change lane
- d   move onto the hard shoulder

Q550

What does this sign mean?

Mark one answer

- a No motor vehicles
- b End of motorway
- c No through road
- d End of bus lane

Q551

Which of these signs means that the national speed limit applies?

Mark one answer

a

b

c

d

Q552

What is the maximum speed on a single carriageway road?

Mark one answer

- a 50 mph
- b 60 mph
- c 40 mph
- d 70 mph

Answers and Explanations

Q429 d

Q430 d

Q431 a Red circles tell you what you must not do. Rectangles usually give you information.

Q432 a

Q433 b This sign means no vehicles except bicycles being pushed by hand.

Q434 d

Q435 b

Q436 d

Q437 d

Q438 d

Q439 a

Q440 c

Q441 b 'c' means no motor vehicles except motorcycles without sidecars.

Q442 a

Q443 b

Q444 a There will also be a plate indicating when the restriction applies.

Q445 d

Q446 b

Q447 b

Q448 b

Q449 c

Q450 c

Q451 a

Q452 c

Q453 c This is a clearway sign and you must not stop at all.

Q454 b

Q455 c

Q456 b You must always stop at a stop sign.

Q457 d

Q458 c

Q459 c

Q460 c

Q461 d

Q462 a

Q463 d

Q464 a

Q465 d Circular signs with blue backgrounds tell you what you must do.

Q466 b

Q467 d

Q468 b

Q469 a

Q470 a

Q471 a

Q472 b

Q473 a

Q474 d

Q475 a, c, e, f

Q476 c

Q477 c

Q478 b

Q479 d

Q480 c

Q481 b

Q482 b Red triangles usually give a warning.

Q483 b

Q484 d

Q485 d

Q486 a

Q487 c

Q488 a

Q489 c

Q490 a

Q491 d

Q492 a

Q493 b

Q494 c

Q495 d The sign is warning of a possible danger ahead so it would be dangerous to overtake.

Q496 c

Q497 c

Q498 d

Q499 c

Q500 a

Q501 a The sequence of traffic lights is red, then red and amber, then green, then amber alone, then red.

Q502 c

Q503 d An amber light means stop, and the lights will next change to red.

Q504 a You must always stop at a red traffic light.

Q505 c The next light will be green and you must wait to drive on until it appears.

Q506 b

Q507 b But also watch for other traffic.

Q508 a

Q509 c

Q510 a

Q511 c

Q512 b, d, f

Q513 a

Q514 b

Q515 a

Q516 c

Q517 c

Q518 b

Q519 b Long lines with short gaps between them in the middle of the road are hazard warning lines. The more paint the more danger.

Q520 b

Q521 c Because the major road is on a bend, your vision is restricted to both left and right.

Q522 a

Q523 b

Q524 d

Q525 a

Q526 b You must stop, but 'c' is wrong because it may not be safe to stop immediately.

Q527 d

Q528 a

Q529 a

Q530 d Then park in a safe place and check your indicators.

Q531 a

Q532 c Sounding your horn has the same meaning as flashing your headlights – to warn of your presence.

Q533 c 'c' is the correct answer because that is what flashing your headlights is supposed to mean. Not everyone knows or obeys the rules and may flash their headlights for other reasons, so always try to make sure of what they mean before you decide on any action.

Q534 b

Q535 b The approaching vehicle might have left the signal on by mistake, or intended to stop after the junction. Always wait long enough to be sure the vehicle is really turning left.

Q536 b Note that the question states 'when driving'. The types of roads in 'b' are the only places where it is legal to use hazard warning lights while your car is moving.

Q537 b

Q538 a You must not overtake on the left on a motorway or dual carriageway unless you are moving in queues of slow-moving traffic.

Q539 a Obviously you must make sure it is safe before doing so.

Q540 b

Q541 d

Q542 c Always look well ahead and you will have plenty of time to react.

Q543 d

Q544 c

Q545 c

Q546 b

Q547 b You must go no further in that lane. You may change lanes and proceed, unless flashing red lights appear above all of them.

Q548 c

Q549 a

Q550 b

Q551 d

Q552 b

Driving Theory Test Questions

Documents

Q553

To drive on the road learners MUST

Mark one answer

- a   have NO penalty points on their licence
- b   have taken professional instruction
- c   have a signed, valid provisional licence
- d   apply for a driving test within 12 months

Q554

For which TWO of these must you show your motor insurance certificate?

Mark two answers

- a   When you are taking your driving test
- b   When buying or selling a vehicle
- c   When a police officer asks you for it
- d   When you are taxing your vehicle
- e   When having an MOT inspection

Q555

A police officer asks to see your driving documents. You do not have them with you. You may produce them at a police station within

Mark one answer

- a   5 days
- b   7 days
- c   14 days
- d   21 days

Q556

Before driving anyone else's motor vehicle you should make sure that

Mark one answer

- a   the vehicle owner has third party insurance cover
- b   your own vehicle has insurance cover
- c   the vehicle is insured for your use
- d   the owner has left the insurance documents in the vehicle

Q557

What is the legal minimum insurance cover you must have to drive on public roads?

Mark one answer

- a   Third party, fire and theft
- b   Fully comprehensive
- c   Third party only
- d   Personal injury cover

Q558

Your car has third party insurance. What does this cover?

Mark three answers

- a   Damage to your own car
- b   Damage to your car by fire
- c   Injury to another person
- d   Damage to someone else's property
- e   Damage to other vehicles
- f   Injury to yourself

Q559

The cost of your insurance will be reduced if

Mark one answer
- a   your car is large and powerful
- b   you are using the car for work purposes
- c   you have penalty points on your licence
- d   you are over 25 years old

Q560

Motor cars and motorcycles must FIRST have an MOT test certificate when they are

Mark one answer
- a   one year old
- b   three years old
- c   five years old
- d   seven years old

Q561

An MOT certificate is normally valid for

Mark one answer
- a   three years after the date it was issued
- b   10,000 miles
- c   one year after the date it was issued
- d   30,000 miles

Q562

When is it legal to drive a car over three years old without an MOT certificate?

Mark one answer
- a   Up to seven days after the old certificate has run out
- b   When driving to an MOT centre to arrange an appointment
- c   Just after buying a second-hand car with no MOT
- d   When driving to an appointment at an MOT centre

Q563

Your vehicle needs a current MOT certificate. You do not have one. Until you do have one you will not be able to renew your

Mark one answer
- a   driving licence
- b   vehicle insurance
- c   road tax disc
- d   vehicle registration document

Q564

Which of these vehicles is not required to have an MOT certificate?

Mark two answers
- a   Police vehicle
- b   Small trailer
- c   Ambulance
- d   Taxi
- e   Caravan

Q565

Which THREE of the following do you need before you can drive legally?

Mark three answers

- a A valid signed driving licence
- b A valid tax disc displayed on your vehicle
- c Proof of your identity
- d A current MOT certificate if the car is over three years old (or four years in Northern Ireland)
- e Fully comprehensive insurance
- f A vehicle handbook

Q566

Which THREE pieces of information are found on a vehicle registration document?

Mark three answers

- a Registered keeper
- b Make of the vehicle
- c Service history details
- d Date of the MOT
- e Type of insurance cover
- f Engine size

Answers and Explanations

Q553 c You are not allowed to drive until you have applied for and received your provisional licence and have signed it in ink.

Q554 c, d

Q555 b You may select the police station of your choice.

Q556 c Your own vehicle insurance may cover you as a passenger in another person's vehicle but very rarely covers you to drive it.

Q557 c This only covers damage to other people and their property.

Q558 c, d, e

Q559 d Drivers over 25 years old have less accidents than younger drivers. As they make fewer insurance claims, the cost of their premiums is usually less.

Q560 b

Q561 c

Q562 d If your car is over three years old and has no valid MOT certificate, you must pre-book an appointment at an MOT centre before you drive it there.

Q563 c When you renew your road tax disc you must produce a valid certificate of insurance and also a current MOT certificate if your car is over three years old.

Q564 b, e

Q565 a, b, d 'e' does not apply because it says fully comprehensive insurance.

Q566 a, b, f

Driving Theory Test Questions

Accident Handling

Q567

You are the first to arrive at the scene of an accident. Which FOUR of these should you do?

Mark four answers

- a   Leave as soon as another motorist arrives
- b   Switch off the vehicle engine(s)
- c   Move uninjured people away from the vehicle(s)
- d   Call the emergency services
- e   Warn other traffic

Q568

You arrive at the scene of a motorcycle accident. The rider is conscious but in shock. You should make sure that

Mark one answer

- a   the rider's helmet is removed
- b   the rider is moved to the side of the road
- c   the rider's helmet is not removed
- d   the rider is put in the recovery position

Q569

You are the first person to arrive at an accident where people are badly injured. Which THREE should you do?

Mark three answers

- a   Switch on your own hazard warning lights
- b   Make sure that someone telephones for an ambulance
- c   Try and get people who are injured to drink something
- d   Move the people who are injured clear of their vehicles
- e   Get people who are not injured clear of the scene

Q570

A tanker is involved in an accident. Which sign would show if the tanker is carrying dangerous goods?

Mark one answer

- a    **LONG VEHICLE**
- b
- c
- d

Q571

You have stopped at the scene of an accident to give help. Which THREE things should you do?

Mark three answers

- a Keep injured people warm and comfortable
- b Keep injured people calm by talking to them reassuringly
- c Keep injured people on the move by walking them around
- d Give injured people a warm drink
- e Make sure that injured people are not left alone

Q572

You have broken down on a two-way road. You have a warning triangle. You should place the warning triangle at least how far from your vehicle?

Mark one answer

- a 5 metres (16 feet)
- b 25 metres (80 feet)
- c 50 metres (165 feet)
- d 100 metres (330 feet)

Q573

While driving, a warning light on your vehicle's instrument panel comes on. You should

Mark one answer

- a continue if the engine sounds alright
- b hope that it is just a temporary electrical fault
- c deal with the problem when there is more time
- d check out the problem quickly and safely

Q574

For which TWO should you use hazard warning lights?

Mark two answers

- a When you slow down quickly on a motorway because of a hazard ahead
- b When you have broken down
- c When you wish to stop on double yellow lines
- d When you need to park on the pavement

Q575

You arrive at the scene of a motorcycle accident. No other vehicle is involved. The rider is unconscious, lying in the middle of the road. The first thing you should do is

Mark one answer

- a move the rider out of the road
- b warn other traffic
- c clear the road of debris
- d give the rider reassurance

Q576

For which THREE should you use your hazard warning lights?

Mark three answers

- a   When you are parking in a restricted area
- b   When you are temporarily obstructing traffic
- c   To warn following traffic of a hazard ahead
- d   When you have broken down

Q577

When are you allowed to use hazard warning lights?

Mark one answer

- a   When stopped and temporarily obstructing traffic
- b   When driving during darkness without headlights
- c   When parked for shopping on double yellow lines
- d   When travelling slowly because you are lost

Q578

When should you switch on your hazard warning lights?

Mark one answer

- a   When you cannot avoid causing an obstruction
- b   When you are driving slowly due to bad weather
- c   When you are towing a broken down vehicle
- d   When you are parked on double yellow lines

Q579

You are in an accident on an 'A' class road. You have a warning triangle with you. At what distance before the obstruction should you place the warning triangle?

Mark one answer

- a   100 metres (330 feet)
- b   50 metres (165 feet)
- c   25 metres (80 feet)
- d   150 metres (492 feet)

Q580

You have broken down on an ordinary road. You have a warning triangle. It should be displayed

Mark one answer

- a   on the roof of your vehicle
- b   at least 150 metres (492 feet) behind your vehicle
- c   at least 50 metres (165 feet) behind your vehicle
- d   just behind your vehicle

Q581

You are involved in a road accident with another driver. Your vehicle is damaged. Which FOUR of the following should you find out?

Mark four answers

- a Whether the driver owns the other vehicle involved
- b The other driver's name, address and telephone number
- c The car make and registration number of the other vehicle
- d The occupation of the other driver
- e The details of the other driver's vehicle insurance
- f Whether the other driver is licensed to drive

Q582

You have an accident while driving and someone is injured. You do not produce your insurance certificate at the time. You must report it to the police as soon as possible, or in any case within

Mark one answer

- a 24 hours
- b 48 hours
- c 5 days
- d 7 days

Q583

At a railway level crossing the red light signal continues to flash after a train has gone by. What should you do?

KEEP CROSSING CLEAR

Mark one answer

- a Phone the signal operator
- b Alert drivers behind you
- c Wait
- d Proceed with caution

Q584

You break down on a level crossing. The lights have not yet begun to flash. Which THREE things should you do?

Mark three answers

- a Telephone the signal operator
- b Leave your vehicle and get everyone clear
- c Walk down the track and signal the next train
- d Move the vehicle if a signal operator tells you to
- e Tell drivers behind what has happened

Q585

You have stalled in the middle of a level crossing and cannot restart the engine. The warning bell starts to ring. You should

Mark one answer

- a   get out and clear of the crossing
- b   run down the track to warn the signalman
- c   carry on trying to restart the engine
- d   push the vehicle clear of the crossing

Q586

Your vehicle has broken down on an automatic railway level crossing. What should you do FIRST?

Mark one answer

- a   Get everyone out of the vehicle and clear of the crossing
- b   Phone the signal operator so that trains can be stopped
- c   Walk along the track to give warning to any approaching trains
- d   Try to push the vehicle clear of the crossing as soon as possible

Q587

Your tyre bursts while you are driving. Which TWO things should you do?

Mark two answers

- a   Pull on the handbrake
- b   Brake as quickly as possible
- c   Pull up slowly at the side of the road
- d   Hold the steering wheel firmly to keep control
- e   Continue on at a normal speed

Q588

Which TWO things should you do when a front tyre bursts?

Mark two answers

- a   Apply the handbrake to stop the vehicle
- b   Brake firmly and quickly
- c   Let the vehicle roll to a stop
- d   Hold the steering wheel lightly
- e   Grip the steering wheel firmly

Q589

Your vehicle has a puncture on a motorway. What should you do?

Mark one answer

- a   Drive slowly to the next service area to get assistance
- b   Pull up on the hard shoulder. Change the wheel as quickly as possible
- c   Pull up on the hard shoulder. Use the emergency phone to get assistance
- d   Switch on your hazard lights. Stop in your lane

Q590

What TWO safeguards could you take against fire risk to your vehicle?

Mark two answers

- a   Keep water levels above maximum
- b   Carry a fire extinguisher
- c   Avoid driving with a full tank of petrol
- d   Use unleaded petrol
- e   Check out any strong smell of petrol
- f   Use low octane fuel

Q591

You are driving on a motorway. A large box falls onto the carriageway from a lorry ahead of you. The lorry does not stop. You should

Mark one answer

- a   drive to the next emergency telephone and inform the police
- b   catch up with the lorry and try to get the driver's attention
- c   stop close to the box and switch on your hazard warning lights until the police arrive
- d   pull over to the hard shoulder, then try and remove the box

Q592

You have broken down on a motorway. When you use the emergency telephone you will be asked

Mark three answers

- a   for the number on the telephone that you are using
- b   for your driving licence details
- c   for the name of your vehicle insurance company
- d   for details of yourself and your vehicle
- e   whether you belong to a motoring organisation

Q593

On the motorway the hard shoulder should be used

Mark one answer

- a   to answer a mobile phone
- b   when an emergency arises
- c   for a short rest when tired
- d   to check a road atlas

Q594

You are on the motorway. Luggage falls from your vehicle. What should you do?

Mark one answer

- a   Stop at the next emergency telephone and contact the police
- b   Stop on the motorway and put on hazard lights whilst you pick it up
- c   Reverse back up the motorway to pick it up
- d   Pull up on the hard shoulder and wave traffic down

Q595

You are driving on a motorway. When can you use hazard warning lights?

Mark two answers

- a   When a vehicle is following too closely
- b   When you slow down quickly because of danger ahead
- c   When you are towing another vehicle
- d   When driving on the hard shoulder
- e   When you have broken down, on the hard shoulder

Answers and Explanations

Q567   b, c, d, e

Q568   c The helmet is giving support in the case of head injury.

Q569   a, b, e

Q570   b

Q571   a, b, e You should not move injured people unless they are in danger; nor should you give them anything to drink.

Q572   c

Q573   d

Q574   a, b

Q575   b Note that this is the FIRST thing to do. By warning other traffic you help reduce the risk of more collisions.

Q576   b, c, d

Q577   a

Q578   a

Q579   b 50 metres is recommended on A roads and 150 metres on motorways and dual carriageways.

Q580   c

Q581   a, b, c, e

Q582   a Note that you have 24 hours in which to report the accident but are allowed up to seven days in which to produce your driving licence, insurance and MOT certificates if required to do so.

Q583   c This usually means another train is coming.

Q584   a, b, d

Q585   a A train may arrive within seconds so 'a' is the only safe possibility.

Q586   a Your first action is to get everyone to safety.

Q587   c, d You will need both hands firmly on the wheel in order to control the car, and using the gears or brakes is likely to make your car swerve. When possible, it is safest just to let your car roll to a halt at the side of the road.

Q588   c, e

Q589   c The hard shoulder of a motorway is a dangerous place and 'c' is the safest course of action. It can be particularly dangerous to try to change an offside wheel as you may be very close to fast-moving traffic in the left-hand lane.

Q590   b, e

Q591   a

Q592   a, d, e

Q593   b

Q594   a

Q595   b, e

Driving Theory Test Questions

Vehicle Loading

Q596

Any load that is carried on a roof rack MUST be

Mark one answer

- ○ a securely fastened when driving
- ○ b carried only when strictly necessary
- ○ c as light as possible
- ○ d covered with plastic sheeting

Q597

When your vehicle is loaded you MUST make sure that the load will

Mark one answer

- ○ a remain secure
- ○ b be easy to unload
- ○ c not be damaged
- ○ d not damage the vehicle

Q598

Which THREE are suitable restraints for a child under three years?

Mark three answers

- ○ a A child seat
- ○ b An adult holding a child
- ○ c An adult seat belt
- ○ d A lap belt
- ○ e A harness
- ○ f A baby carrier

Q599

Your car is fitted with child safety door locks. When used this means that normally

Mark one answer

- ○ a the rear doors can only be opened from the outside
- ○ b the rear doors can only be opened from the inside
- ○ c all the doors can only be opened from the outside
- ○ d all the doors can only be opened from the inside

Q600

What do child locks in a vehicle do?

Mark one answer

- ○ a Lock the seat belt buckles in place
- ○ b Lock the rear windows in the up position
- ○ c Stop children from opening rear doors
- ○ d Stop the rear seats from tipping forward

Q601

Your vehicle is fitted with child safety door locks. You should use these so that children inside the car cannot open

Mark one answer

- ○ a the right-hand doors
- ○ b the left-hand doors
- ○ c the rear doors
- ○ d any of the doors

Q602

Would it be safe to allow children to sit BEHIND the rear seats of a hatchback car?

Mark one answer

- a Yes, if you can see clearly to the rear
- b Yes, if they're under 11 years
- c No, unless all the other seats are full
- d No, not in any circumstances

Q603

You should load a trailer so that the weight is

Mark one answer

- a mostly over the nearside wheel
- b evenly distributed
- c mainly at the front
- d mostly at the rear

Q604

Before towing a caravan you should ensure that heavy items in it are loaded

Mark one answer

- a as high as possible, mainly over the axle(s)
- b as low as possible, mainly over the axle(s)
- c as low as possible, forward of the axle(s)
- d as high as possible, forward of the axle(s)

Q605

If a trailer swerves or snakes when you are towing it you should

Mark one answer

- a ease off the accelerator and reduce your speed
- b let go of the steering wheel and let it correct itself
- c brake hard and hold the pedal down
- d increase your speed as quickly as possible

Q606

Are passengers allowed to ride in a caravan that is being towed?

Mark one answer

- a Yes
- b No
- c Only if all the seats in the towing vehicle are full
- d Only if a stabilizer is fitted

Q607

You are towing a trailer and experience snaking. How would you reduce it?

Mark one answer

- a Ease off the accelerator slowly
- b Press the accelerator firmly
- c Steer sharply
- d Brake hard

Q608

How can you stop a caravan snaking from side to side?

Mark one answer

- a Turn the steering wheel slowly to each side
- b Accelerate to increase your speed
- c Stop as quickly as you can
- d Slow down very gradually

Q609

You are towing a small trailer on a busy three-lane motorway. All the lanes are open. You must

Mark two answers

- a not exceed 60 mph
- b not overtake
- c have a stabilizer fitted
- d use only the left and centre lanes

Answers and Explanations

Q596 **a** The word 'MUST' in the question makes 'a' correct.

Q597 **a**

Q598 **a, e, f**

Q599 **a**

Q600 **c** Child locks prevent the rear doors being opened from the inside.

Q601 **c**

Q602 **d** The area behind the rear seats of a hatchback car is designed to crumple in the event of a collision and is therefore not a safe place in which to sit.

Q603 **b** This creates the greatest stability.

Q604 **b** This reduces the risk of the caravan swerving about or being top heavy and tipping over.

Q605 **a** Options 'b', 'c' or 'd' would all be likely to make the problem worse.

Q606 **b**

Q607 **a**

Q608 **d**

Q609 **a, d**

Driving Theory Test Questions

Notes

NOTES

NOTES

NOTES

For information on learning to drive with a BSM instructor please contact your local BSM centre free on:

0800 700 800

BSM instructors operate under a franchise with
The British School of Motoring Limited, the largest organisation of its kind
in the world.

 *The pass masters*

The two additional books in the series, *Pass Your Driving Test* and *Pass Your Driving Theory Test*, are available from all BSM centres and from most good bookshops.

The pass masters

FIRST AID
IS A SKILL FOR LIFE – LITERALLY...

The actions of the first person on the scene of an accident can be a matter of life or death for the victims – would you be prepared?

- Each subject is fully illustrated with colour photographs
- Technical drawings probe beneath the surface
- Signs and symptoms are given for speedy recognition
- Easy-to-follow step-by-step procedures for treatment
- Warning boxes draw attention to vital points
- Includes 16-page Emergency Index for quick reference

First Aid for Motorists has step-by-step advice on what to do at an emergency, and gives clear guidance on the simple life-saving techniques that every motorist should know.
Available from all good bookshops now.